D0575340

$3

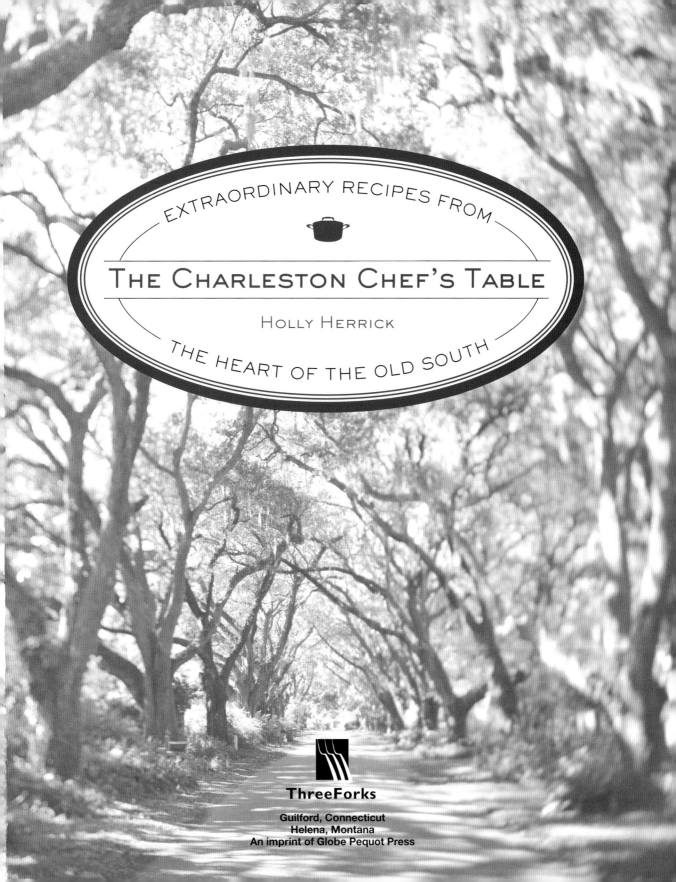

EXTRAORDINARY RECIPES FROM

THE CHARLESTON CHEF'S TABLE

HOLLY HERRICK

THE HEART OF THE OLD SOUTH

ThreeForks

Guilford, Connecticut
Helena, Montana
An imprint of Globe Pequot Press

To buy books in quantity for corporate use
or incentives, call **(800) 962–0973**
or e-mail **premiums@GlobePequot.com.**

ThreeForks®

Copyright © 2010 by Holly Herrick

ALL RIGHTS RESERVED. No part of this book may be reproduced or transmitted in any form by any means, electronic or mechanical, including photocopying and recording, or by any information storage and retrieval system, except as may be expressly permitted in writing from the publisher. Requests for permission should be addressed to Globe Pequot Press, Attn: Rights and Permissions Department, P.O. Box 480, Guilford, CT 06437.

ThreeForks is a registered trademark of Morris Book Publishing, LLC.

"Seaside Similes" by S. Lewis Johnson, *Sparks from My Chimney,* copyright © 1963. Reprinted by permission of Kathleen Johnson Hall.

Crab soup recipe from *Amazing Grace: A Collection of Recipes from Grace Episcopal Church,* Charleston, South Carolina, copyright © 2007. Reprinted and adapted by permission of Mary Bradley and Grace Episcopal Church.

Project editor: David Legere
Text design: Libby Kingsbury
Layout artist: Nancy Freeborn
Photos by Christopher Brown

Library of Congress Cataloging-in-Publication Data
Herrick, Holly.
  The Charleston chef's table : extraordinary recipes from the heart of the Old South / Holly Herrick.
      p. cm.
  ISBN 978-0-7627-5010-8
  1. Restaurants—South Carolina—Charleston—Guidebooks. 2. Cookery—South Carolina—Charleston.
I. Title.
  TX907.3.S6732H47 2010
  641.59757—dc22
                                                                                    2009030309

Printed in China
10 9 8 7 6 5 4 3 2

To my parents, Herbert and Margaret McCauley,
and my former husband and good friend, Greg Herrick.
Thank you for always supporting my dreams and unselfishly providing
a strong education at both Boston College and Le Cordon Bleu,
which helped these dreams become realities.

CONTENTS

Acknowledgments

After nearly a decade of living and working in Charleston as a restaurant critic and food writer, I haven't been able to decide if the food here tastes so good because Charleston is just so darn beautiful or if it's because Charleston's beauty attracts so many wonderful chefs. Isn't beauty drawn to beauty? Is it cause or effect? Thankfully, these questions don't really demand answers. Instead, we're all invited to sit back and reap the gorgeous gustatory rewards.

And so I extend a huge and hearty thank-you to Charleston and to all of the city's dedicated and talented chefs who give of themselves daily to produce artistry in their kitchens. Without their generosity, this book would not have been possible. Thank you all for answering my questions and providing tested recipes for some of your most celebrated dishes. It's been truly fun getting to know all of you better.

Also, special thanks to my editor at Globe Pequot Press, Heather Carreiro. She believed in this book even before I did and stood by me through the long journey to making it a reality. Christopher Brown, the photographer for this book, was an absolute joy to work with and took pictures that do justice to arguably one of the most beautiful places on earth and to the people and food that help make her that way. Thank you, Chris.

All my dedicated tasters and food-scouting companions—Bates, Phil, Richard—thank you. As delicious as most of the meals were, eating and analyzing food for a living is work. You always made it feel more like play.

Thank you to all my friends, family, and neighbors who listened to me talking about this for as long as I did and for walking me through occasional bouts of deadline panic.

Finally, my canine angel, Tann Mann, thank you for just being sweet, chocolate you.

Introduction

As American author, poet, and Charleston native DuBose Heyward wrote in "Dusk," a poem to Charleston, she is indeed "alone among the cities." Her haunting colonial and antebellum architectural curves and the luscious winding waterways that embrace her would be enough for Charleston to claim a unique beauty and presence. But there is much more. A big part of Charleston's radiance is her delicious status as one of this country's most popular dining and tourist destinations. Charleston ranked number two among *Condé Nast Traveler* magazine's top ten travel destinations in 2008, while readers of *Travel and Leisure* ranked Charleston as the fourth best city in America that year. In addition, the U.S. Census Bureau reports that the population of the Charleston metro area has surged 35.6 percent since 1980, adding fuel to the growing appetite for good food among locals.

To understand the general and culinary present, we have to look briefly to the past. Unlike the other American colonies, Charleston, founded in 1670, was chartered by fun-loving, party-hearty King Charles II of England, and before long the young town embraced religious tolerance for its residents. Immigrants from England were looking for a chance to prosper and have a good time like the wealthy landowners of Merry England, while many immigrants from France, Ireland, Scotland, and elsewhere came to escape religious persecution. Thus, unlike Quaker Philadelphia and Puritan Boston, Charleston, also known as "The Holy City," was home to a cultural and culinary mix, one that was infinitely larger (it had, for example, the biggest French population of any colony), more complex, and arguably more sophisticated than her colonial contemporaries.

But it was the Lowcountry—a sixty-mile stretch of low-lying land that includes Charleston—whose geography, marshes, and tidal-driven interchanges of fresh and salt water led to the city's largest and most tragic immigration. Slaves, mostly from the rice-producing region of Sierra Leone in Africa, came to the port city by the thousands to help planters grow and harvest rice crops that quickly made Charleston one of the country's wealthiest cities, a status she held until the Civil War. Like the French, Jews, and Scottish Baptists, the Africans brought with them a taste for the flavors and ingredients of their homelands, including okra, rice, and field peas. Unlike slaves in other colonies, slaves in this area worked on a task system. They were allowed and encouraged to work their own private gardens and do their own cooking, according to historian Robert Stockton. In this way, the slaves preserved their own culinary traditions, traditions that would later trickle down into Charleston's culinary mix, in dishes like gumbo and hoppin' John.

In this solitary melting pot of wealth and sophistication, a cornucopia of seafood and produce ingredients and an early-established insatiability for good food and good times endure to this day. In Charleston, one does not get "drunk" or "hung over" but instead "over served." But what and where Charlestonians and visitors eat have changed since days past—especially in the last twenty-five years.

Long saddled with episodes of poverty, devastating hurricanes, and earthquakes and fires (especially after the Civil War), Charlestonians developed a driving sense of survival, pride, and practicality. These qualities led them to preserve many of the historic structures—and the endearing Southern charm—that would eventually bring the tourists, the money, and the vast pool of delicious restaurants Charleston now enjoys.

Charleston's culinary and cultural evolution came in three distinct waves. Long-time resident and author Barbara Hagerty describes Charleston between World War II and the late seventies as "backwater" or "provincial," offering only two restaurants of note. The first wave of change began in 1977, when Gian Carlo Menotti chose Charleston as the site of what would become a wildly successful annual art and cultural festival, Spoleto USA. At about the same time, newly elected Charleston mayor Joseph P. Riley undertook extensive and successful efforts to rejuvenate the dilapidated downtown shopping area, creating the Charleston Place shopping center and a luxury hotel. Both proved to be magnets for tourists, and the new culinary and hospitality school Johnson & Wales (now located in Charlotte, North Carolina) would train chefs like Peninsula Grill's Robert Carter to feed the rapidly evolving gustatory appetites of tourists and locals alike.

The next wave of change came in the aftermath of a tragedy, Hurricane Hugo, on September 21, 1989. "Relief poured in from around the nation and the world, both in volunteers and funds. Insurance companies, some of which went out of business because of Hugo, paid over $3.2 billion in claims," writes local historian, Robert Rosen, in his book *A Short History of Charleston* (University of South Carolina Press, 1997). In the storm's aftermath, groundbreaking Southern chefs like Magnolia's Donald Barickman and Slightly North of Broad's Frank Lee seized the opportunity to show the world the wonders of grits prepared with cream and the sultriness of real she-crab soup. South Carolina native Frank Lee even introduced something relatively exotic to Charleston at the time—pad thai. Famous movies like *North and South* and *The Prince of Tides;* a literary renaissance through the works of Pat Conroy, Dottie Frank, and Alexandra Ripley; and a fat money trail of the super-rich leading to downtown and the resort islands of Kiawah, Seabrook, and Wild Dunes, followed.

Drawn by Charleston's magnetic force, I moved here from Jackson Hole, Wyoming, in 2000 to be a restaurant critic for *The Post and Courier.* Charleston was already smoking hot in the food department. But in the ten years since, she has become an absolute culinary mecca. Approximately half of the restaurants in this book were not around in 2000, and those that were are constantly improving to stay at the top of their game. New chefs like McCrady's Sean Brock have brought sophisticated innovation through sous vide technique, spinning it with the homespun goodness of vegetables he raises in his own garden. Hominy Grill's Robert Stehling was named Southeast Chef of the Year in 2008, FIG's Mike Lata was named Southeast Chef of the Year in 2009, and many more, from Bob Waggoner to Lauren Mitterer, have received James Beard nominations. Charleston's annual Food & Wine Festival (founded in 2006) is another testimony to how utterly edible Charleston has become.

This book was written to celebrate beautiful Charleston and her extraordinarily talented chefs from restaurants small and large, simple and fancy. Restaurants were chosen for inclusion based first and foremost on the high quality of the food they consistently deliver but also for their unique personalities. Recipes run the gamut from ultrasimple six-ingredient soups, like Alluette's Café's simply delicious Lima Bean Soup, to the intricacies of Red Orchid's recipe for plump and tasty Barbecue Pork Buns. Feel free to make them just as the chefs do or to modify them and make them your own. One caveat: Always taste and season carefully as you work. It's essential to good cooking.

All of the restaurants featured in *The Charleston Chef's Table* are located within a thirty-mile radius of the downtown peninsula. Most are located on or near the peninsula or in nearby suburbs like West Ashley and Mount Pleasant. This book is intended to be as much a recipe book for cooking enthusiasts as an ode to Charleston for those who love her from afar, for those who have been lucky enough to visit, and perhaps for the luckiest of all—those who call Charleston home. Please think of these recipes and the fabulous photography by Christopher Brown as a gracious invitation, extended directly to you, to visit and taste beautiful Charleston, literally and figuratively. For that is the intention behind the words on the pages that follow.

We nod to greet some friends we meet

As through wrought iron gate

We slowly pass bright polished brass,

And hope that we are late.

Like honey bees in acacia trees

Distant voices hum,

And from within, a merry din,

As nearer the house we come

People stand like steeples,

High-ball ice-chimes in hand,

Like buoy bells the tinkling swells

Across the social strand.

"Seaside Similes" by S. Lewis Johnson, *Sparks from My Chimney,* copyright © 1963. Reprinted by permission of the author's daughter, Kathleen Johnson Hall.

Starters

Since the city's earliest days, Charlestonians have reveled in the pleasures of petite bites paired with libations. While then it was often port or Madeira with cheese sticks or benne wafers, these days the choices are considerably vaster and decidedly more international. Whether at home or at restaurants, Charlestonians whet their appetites while wetting their whistles with a plethora of small plates or tapas paired with just the right drink.

Ponder La Fourchette's creamy, dreamy, and consummately French Coquilles St. Jacques à la Bretagne with a cool glass of Muscadet. Or Red Orchid's sweet, spicy Barbecue Pork Buns with a dry sip of sake. Or Chai's Lounge and Tapas Krystal-gone-gourmet Mini Angus Burgers and Med-Bistro's hearty, irresistible House Chips with Blue Cheese Fondue with an earthy, ice-cold brew. For Peninsula Grill's smart and ultimately Southern Seared Foie Gras with Black Pepper–Duck Biscuits and Carolina Peach Jam, it's got to be a flute of the house's best champagne.

Jestine's Kitchen

251 Meeting Street, downtown
(843) 722-7224
Owner: Dana Berlin Strange

Six mornings of every week of the year, the line at the corner of Wentworth and Meeting Streets forms. It begins with a murmuring cluster of curious first-timers and loyal regulars, at just about 10:45 a.m., and grows into a mostly polite clamor by 11:00 a.m. when Jestine's doors open, revealing the soulful Southern haven that has matured in a little less than fifteen years to a Charleston institution.

Opened in part as a communal legacy for owner Dana Berlin Strange's childhood nanny, Jestine Matthews, the restaurant steadily cranks out the kind of food that Dana and three generations of her family enjoyed under Jestine's loving care. Though Jestine passed at the ripe old age of 112 more than a decade ago, her spirit and hospitality truly do live on at Jestine's.

Dana reserves a few seats in the back for regulars, but the space teems with those who have come from near and far to savor Jestine's towering plate of fried chicken and top it off with airy coconut cream pie—the real custard, real whipped cream, and house-made pastry variety—washed down with sweet tea or Jestine's "table wine."

Instead of bread, every meal at Jestine's begins with a petite diner-style bowl of cool, refreshing Refrigerator Pickles. "My mom and grandmother made them regularly when we were growing up," says Dana. After a night in the fridge, fresh "garden variety" cucumbers are transformed into crisp slivers of Southern goodness. Eat them up quickly, however, because they get too soft after three or four days, according to Dana.

Refrigerator Pickles

(Makes 1 quart or approximately 8 appetizer portions)

2 medium cucumbers, cut in half lengthwise and
   thinly sliced
1 onion, halved and thinly sliced
2 tablespoons whole black peppercorns
¼ cup white wine vinegar
¼ cup granulated sugar
Pinch of salt

Special equipment: 1 quart-size glass Mason
   (or another brand) jar

In a medium bowl, toss together the cucumbers, onion, and peppercorns. Pack them loosely in the quart-size jar. Combine the vinegar, sugar, and salt in a separate small bowl, whisking to combine. Pour the vinegar mixture into the jar, covering the cucumbers and onion. (Note: You may have a little more or less vinegar mixture than you need depending on the size of the cucumbers. The ratio of vinegar to sugar is always the same—50/50—so whip up more if you need it.) Seal the jar and refrigerate overnight or up to 12 hours. "Taste the next morning and if they are not sweet enough, add a little more sugar," says Dana. Serve immediately, while still cold.

FAT HEN

3140 MAYBANK HIGHWAY, JOHNS ISLAND
(843) 559-9090
WWW.THEFATHEN.COM
CHEF-OWNER: FRED NEUVILLE

Follow your nose and the red chicken tracks on the front porch of this restaurant roost with Lowcountry/French Huguenot–inspired pluck. Fat Hen's "coop" has a convenient Johns Island address, situated virtually equidistant from downtown and the upscale resort barrier islands Kiawah and Seabrook. Congenial chef-owner Fred Neuville is a veteran chef and a graduate of the Culinary Institute of America. He draws heavily on French classical technique and the ingredients indigenous to the Lowcountry at Fat Hen—so named because Fred wanted something that evoked nurturing images and a French undertone. Plus, it's so much fun to say!

Fat Hen lays all kinds of golden dishes, from succulent Short Ribs Braised in a Rich Veal Broth to Seared Duck Leg and Thigh Served with Butter Beans and Garlic Spinach. The sophisticated yet homey French country look and smashing food draw an eclectic, animated crowd. "Our price structure is such that we get the full gamut," says Fred. "People drink Bud Light and people drink Cristal champagne."

His oyster recipe (the fifth-biggest seller at the restaurant) was something he created many years ago, as a young chef working at a French bistro in Richmond, Virginia. He resurrected it at Fat Hen because it was a natural fit with the restaurant's theme. "Oysters and country ham are very Lowcountry and the preparation ties in the French angle. The French have their hams, too," says Fred.

OYSTERS SAUTÉED WITH COUNTRY HAM AND WILD MUSHROOMS OVER GRILLED BREAD

(Serves 4)

4 thick slices Tuscan or country-style bread
2 tablespoons olive oil
½ cup finely chopped shallots
½ cup dry white wine
3 egg yolks
¼ cup heavy cream
¾ cup sliced wild mushrooms (cremini, portobello, shiitake, or a combination)

¾ cup finely cubed aged and cured country ham
½ cup coarsely chopped fresh spinach
20 oysters, shucked
Salt and freshly ground black pepper to taste
Fresh parsley or thyme, chopped (optional)

Heat the oven broiler or grill. Brush both sides of the bread evenly with a thin coating of olive oil. Broil until lightly browned on both sides or grill until just charred. Set aside.

For the topping, heat a large sauté pan over high heat. Add the shallots and the wine and reduce by half. Meanwhile, in a small bowl, combine the egg yolks and heavy cream to create the "liaison." Reduce the heat to medium-low. Add the liaison, mushrooms, and country ham to the pan, and stir occasionally. Once the sauce has thickened and coats the back of a wooden spoon (about 4 minutes), add the spinach and the oysters to the pan. Sauté, stirring, until the oysters just turn translucent and the spinach has wilted, about 3 minutes, depending on the size of the oysters. Season to taste with salt and pepper. Serve over the warm grilled bread, dividing the pan sauce evenly. If desired, garnish with parsley or thyme.

HUGUENOT HAVEN

During long stretches of the sixteenth and seventeenth centuries, Huguenots (French Protestants and members of the Reformed Church established in 1550 by John Calvin) were persecuted in their predominantly Catholic home country of France for following their beliefs. The tension and bloodshed reached an all-time high with Louis XIV's revocation of the Edict of Nantes (1685), which essentially called for the obliteration of the Huguenots. Those who could fled to safe havens, including the thousands who made it to the shores of America between 1618 and 1725. Charleston, unlike Quaker-rich Philadelphia and Puritan-rich Boston, was a religiously tolerant colony that welcomed virtually all religions and was a popular Huguenot immigration destination. The Huguenot legacy here is not a small one; it lives on in old Charleston family names, like Ravenel and Manigault, and in revered dishes, like Huguenot torte and pilau (Huguenot rice pilaf). Incidentally, the Charleston word for *recipe* ("receipt") is derived from the French equivalent *recette*.

RED ORCHID

1401 SAM RITTENBERG BOULEVARD, WEST ASHLEY
(843) 573-8787
OWNERS: TONY AND KELLY CHU

Despite Red Orchid's humble exterior and non-glamorous suburban shopping mall setting, those who enter are treated to an emperor-worthy authentic Chinese dining experience. Husband-and-wife team Tony and Kelly Chu are both natives of China, and they succeed in making the customer number one and the food (with nods from Singapore, Hunan, Szechuan, Shanghai, and Guangzhou) as good as it gets.

Tony rules the front of the house, happily sharing his friendly grace and expert knowledge and collection of sake. Meanwhile, Kelly oversees the back of the house and is referred to as a "master saucer" because of her saucy sauce skills.

Known as *char siu bao* in Chinese, these divine bites of sweet and savory barbecued pork wrapped in a pillowy, dumpling-type dough can best be described as Chinese Sloppy Joes. "Barbecue is one of the many staples on hand at Chinese dim sum shops—which are something like coffee shops that serve tapas-like treats," says Tony. This delectable dish transports him to memories of his childhood, when he regularly supped on the buns with his family. In Tony's version, the dumplings are baked, but they can also be steamed.

Be patient with this recipe. It looks complicated and time-consuming, but if you break it down into three prep parts over the course of a day, it's not hard at all and well worth the effort.

BARBECUE PORK BUNS

(Makes 16 buns)

For the barbecue pork:

2 pounds pork butt, cut into 1-inch cubes
1½ tablespoons each of dark soy sauce,
    light soy sauce, honey, and oyster sauce
2 tablespoons whiskey
3½ tablespoons hoisin sauce
½ teaspoon five-spice powder
¼ teaspoon salt
Pinch of freshly ground black pepper

For the barbecue sauce:

1 tablespoon peanut or vegetable oil
⅔ cup chopped onion
1 cup of the roasted pork
2 teaspoons Chinese rice wine or sherry
4 teaspoons oyster sauce
1 teaspoon sesame oil

1½ teaspoons dark soy sauce
4 teaspoons ketchup
1 tablespoon granulated sugar
6 tablespoons chicken stock
Pinch of freshly ground black pepper

For the dough:

½ cup plus 2 tablespoons granulated sugar
⅔ cup warm water (around 75°F)
3 teaspoons dry active yeast
2⅔ cups high-gluten flour (look for flour
    labeled "best for bread machines")
½ cup (minus 2 tablespoons) peanut or
    vegetable oil
1 egg, beaten, for glazing

To prepare the barbecue pork, toss the pork with the remaining barbecue pork ingredients in a large bowl, working well with your hands to coat evenly. Marinate the pork, covered and refrigerated, for 4 hours or overnight. When ready to cook the pork, preheat the oven broiler and place the oven rack in the position second closest to the broiler. Remove the pork from the marinade (reserve the marinade for basting) and place it in a sturdy roasting pan. Broil for 8 minutes, baste with the marinade, and turn the meat. Repeat this for 20 or 30 minutes, basting and turning the meat every 8 minutes, or until the pork's interior is no longer pink and has reached an internal temperature of 170°F. Tony advises being extra careful not to let the sugar in the marinade char while broiling. Allow the pork to cool and refrigerate, covered, 4 hours or overnight. After the pork has rested, chop it coarsely to create small, Sloppy Joe–size pieces.

To make the sauce and the filling, reserve 1 cup of pork (keep the rest for a second batch or for another use). Heat the oil in a large sauté pan over medium heat. Add the onion and sauté, stirring, until golden brown, about 5 minutes. Add the reserved pork and the remaining sauce ingredients to the pan. Stir together and sauté for another 5 minutes or until fragrant. Reduce the heat to low and simmer until the sauce has reduced to a thick and bubbly consistency. Cool and refrigerate 4 hours or overnight.

To prepare the dough, dissolve the sugar in the warm (not hot!) water in a large bowl. Add the yeast, stir gently, and set aside for 30 minutes to proof. When the mixture is foamy or light brown in color, it's ready. Add the flour and oil to the bowl. With your hands, mix the ingredients together until cohesive. When the dough has formed a ball, remove it from the bowl and knead on a floured surface until smooth and elastic, about 5 minutes. Place the dough in a large, lightly oiled bowl and allow to rise for 4 hours covered loosely with a damp towel.

To make the *bao* balls, lightly flour a working surface and roll the dough out ¼ inch thick. With a 3-inch round cookie cutter, cut out 16 rounds of dough. To fill, scoop a tablespoon of the prepared filling into the center of each dough round. Pull two of the edges together toward the center to cover the filling, and pinch to seal. Turn the dough a quarter turn and pinch the other two edges together. Repeat twice, turning and pinching the

edges, until the bun is sealed, twisting gently the fourth time to ensure that the bun is completely sealed. Repeat with the remaining dough rounds.

Arrange the buns 3 inches apart on a large baking sheet. Set aside to rest and rise until puffy, about 1 hour. Preheat the oven to 350°F. Brush the top of each bun with the beaten egg. Bake for 15 to 20 minutes or until golden brown. Serve immediately.

Monza

451 King Street, downtown
(843) 720-8787
www.monzapizza.com
Executive Chef: Dusty Chorvat

The Ferrari of authentic Neapolitan-style pizza in greater Charleston, Monza reaches an edible finish line with Formula One fare and unparalleled pizza pizzazz. Named after a great Italian car racing track and decked with Italian trimmings, including vintage black-and-white photos of racing greats and a genuine Ferrari engine hoisted over a festive community table, Monza looks the sleek Speed Racer part. Tangerine-colored imported Italian tiles dress the walls, while shiny zebrawood tables swirl together like a giant bowl of ice cream, with warm chocolate and caramel wood tones.

Unlike most pizza joints around town, Monza refuses to deliver and allows precious few menu modifications, all in a winning effort to attract a sophisticated crowd. Occupying the center of Monza's universe is a wood-burning oven that operates at 800°F and eternally emits fragrant white oak smoke. The aroma wafts temptingly down King Street, attracting loyal legions like bees to honey.

Executive chef Dusty Chorvat studied at the Art Institute of Atlanta, later honing a passion for vegetarian and health-oriented food. He puts his passion to good use at Monza in dishes like Marinated Beet and Arugula Salad and Wood-Roasted Asparagus Salad. "I like to make food that's simply prepared and that makes me and others feel good to eat it," he says. The ultimate feel-good food, Monza's ricotta meatballs served in a fresh sauce laced with Italian sausage and red peppers are one example of Dusty's clean interpretation of good cooking. Don't forget fresh bread for dipping, and you've got a meal to remember all in one bowl.

Italian Sausage and Ricotta Meatballs with Peppers, Onions, and Red Wine Sauce

(Serves 4 to 6)

For the sauce:

2 tablespoons extra-virgin olive oil
3 cups chopped onion
3 cups chopped red bell peppers
3 cloves garlic, minced
Salt and freshly ground black pepper to taste
1 cup red wine
2 cups pureed whole peeled canned tomatoes
4 cups hand-crushed whole peeled canned
    tomatoes

For the meatballs:

2 cups fresh bread crumbs (preferably from chewy,
    Tuscan-style bread)
½ cup ricotta cheese
½ cup whole milk
¼ cup chopped fresh flat-leaf parsley
1 large egg
¼ cup grated Parmesan cheese, plus more
    for garnish
1 pound Italian pork sausage, casings removed
Fresh basil to garnish

To make the sauce, heat the olive oil in a large pot over medium heat. Add the onions and peppers and sauté, stirring, until softened, about 8 minutes. Add the garlic and continue to sauté until just softened, about 4 minutes. Season with salt and pepper. Increase heat to high and add the wine. Cook until reduced by about half and you can no longer smell the alcohol. Add the tomatoes and bring to a boil, then reduce to a simmer; continue simmering for another 10 minutes. Season to taste with salt and pepper.

Meanwhile, prepare the meatballs. Preheat the oven to 400°F. In a large bowl, combine the bread crumbs, ricotta, milk, parsley, egg, and Parmesan, mixing well to combine with a wooden spoon. Add the sausage and mix, using your hands, until combined. (Dusty warns against overworking once adding the sausage, or the meatballs risk becoming tough.) Dampen your hands and begin forming golf ball–sized meatballs (approximately 2 ounces each; you should end up with about 16). The meatballs should be slightly sticky. If they are too dry, add a little more milk; if too wet, add a few more bread crumbs. Line a large baking sheet with a sheet of parchment paper and evenly space the meatballs. Bake for 20 minutes or until they're golden brown and firm to the touch. Then add the meatballs to the sauce and simmer another 20 minutes.

Serve meatballs and sauce in shallow bowls and garnish with additional Parmesan cheese and torn basil. This is also delicious over your favorite cooked pasta.

RAVAL

453 KING STREET, DOWNTOWN
(843) 853-8466
WWW.RAVALWINEBAR.COM
EXECUTIVE CHEF: DUSTY CHORVAT

Though next door to Monza, Raval crosses an altogether different European country's border, delivering the distinct moods and flavors of Spain. A spot-on rendition of a Spanish tapas bar, Raval emits the antique spirit of Barcelona. Dark imported wood and flickering candles on gargantuan metal chandeliers set a romantic Moorish tempo, ideal for sipping from Raval's extensive Spanish wine list and nibbling tasty bites. Afterward, retreat through the massive wooden double doors to the padded, Bohemian confines of Raval's back room (weekends only), which rocks with youthful late-night energy.

Great food is not the only thing Monza and Raval have in common. Both (as well as Poe's Tavern, page 90) are owned by restaurant group REV Foods, and the talented Dusty Chorvat commands both kitchens. Though he recently abbreviated the tapas menu, Dusty says Patatas Bravas will always be on the menu. Take one bite and you'll understand why. Revel in the plump fried squares bursting with starchy, russet potato splendor, which reach a texture and flavor crescendo when paired with cool garlic aioli and lip-smacking spicy tomato dipping sauce.

PATATAS BRAVAS WITH AIOLI AND SPICY TOMATO DIPPING SAUCE
(Serves 4 to 6)

For the aioli:

2 large egg yolks (preferably from free-range eggs)
1 tablespoon Dijon mustard
1 tablespoon fresh-squeezed lemon juice
4 cloves roasted garlic, finely minced
¼ cup olive oil
Salt and freshly ground black pepper to taste

For the dipping sauce:

1 cup whole peeled canned tomatoes (Dusty suggests Cento brand)
Generous pinch of red pepper flakes
Salt and freshly ground black pepper to taste

For the potatoes:

4 large russet potatoes, peeled
2 cups peanut oil
½ teaspoon Spanish paprika
Generous sprinkle of salt and freshly ground black pepper to taste

You can make the sauces up to 3 days before serving and keep them refrigerated. To prepare the aioli, whisk together the egg yolks, mustard, lemon juice, and garlic in a medium bowl. Very gradually, drizzle in the olive oil, continuing to whisk vigorously until the aioli reaches a creamy, mayonnaise-like consistency. Season to taste with salt and pepper. Cover and refrigerate until ready to use.

Meanwhile, prepare the dipping sauce. In the bowl of a food processor, combine the tomatoes and red pepper flakes and pulse until smooth. Transfer to a small saucepan and simmer on medium-low for 5 minutes to develop the sauce's flavors. Taste and season as needed with salt and pepper. Cover and refrigerate until ready to use. (About an hour before serving, remove the covered sauce containers from the refrigerator and allow to come to room temperature—the temperature at which they should be served for maximum flavor.)

Then prepare the potatoes. It's important they be cut to a uniform size so they all cook in the same amount of time; it also makes for a prettier presentation. Raval cuts them into fat square slices, but cubes are easier. To make cubes, cut each potato in half vertically, and repeat with each half. Now cut across these lengths, cutting in ½-inch segments. Now cut across the lengths to form ½-inch cubes. Discard any little odd-shaped tidbits or save them for a soup or another use. When you're ready to fry, pour the peanut oil into a deep heavy-bottomed frying pan. Heat over medium-high heat until the temperature reaches 325°F. Place the potatoes in the pan, and parcook for 2 minutes. (Don't crowd the potatoes: They should be fully submerged in the oil. Cook in two batches if necessary.) With a slotted spoon, remove the potatoes and drain on paper towels. Increase the heat and let the oil temperature come to 365°F. Fry the potatoes a second time (cooking twice ensures a crispier fry), until crispy and golden brown, 6 to 8 minutes. Remove

potatoes with a slotted spoon and drain. Toss with the Spanish paprika and salt and pepper. Serve immediately on a platter, with small bowls of the aioli and sauce nearby for dipping.

CHARLESTON GRILL

205 Meeting Street, downtown
(843) 722-4900 or (888) 635-2350
www.charlestonplace.com
Executive Chef: Michelle Weaver

After twelve years working and learning alongside marquee chef Bob Waggoner, Michelle Weaver was given the chance in 2009 to step into the limelight as executive chef at Charleston Grill. In a move that shocked everyone (including Weaver), Waggoner announced his departure to pursue a career in television and other related endeavors. "He has been my mentor, my friend, my family," says Michelle. "Bob was the person who introduced me to my first truffle and French cheese." But Michelle's got big plans for an exciting future at Charleston Grill. Her creativity was the conceptual drive behind the menu she co-created with Waggoner. Weaver's four-part pure, lush, cosmopolitan, and Southern menu was created to allow more diversity at the restaurant. "We needed Southern, simplistic food on the 'Southern' side, Bob's lush French flavors on the 'pure' side, and something more forward-thinking with the 'cosmopolitan' side," says Michelle. She's especially inspired by the "cosmopolitan" section of the menu, for which she finds some "crazy, new" ingredient like yuzu and puts it to work in a delicious, brand-new way.

The relaxed elegance of the mahogany walls, cream-colored leather seating, and sashay of gossamer curtains in the dining room, the top-notch service, and an incredible wine list make Charleston Grill a premier destination for high-level dining. The recipe that follows is a beautiful and delicious example of culinary artistry, with its taste dance of baby beets, fresh orange juice, and tangy goat cheese.

ROASTED GOLDEN BEETS AND CAROLINA GOAT CHEESE

(Serves 4)

For the goat cheese "topper":

10 ounces excellent-quality artisan goat cheese
　　(Weaver uses Anderson Carolina farm's)
4 shallots, finely chopped
½ tablespoon salt
Freshly ground black pepper to taste
6 tablespoons heavy cream

For the sauce:

4½ cups fresh-squeezed orange juice

For the beets:

20 small golden (or purple) beets, skin on and
　　scrubbed, ¼ inch of the stems left clean and
　　intact
½ cup extra-virgin olive oil
4 cups fresh-squeezed orange juice

For serving:

1 cup fresh mâche
Salt and freshly ground black pepper to taste

First, prepare the goat cheese mixture. In a large bowl, gently crumble the goat cheese and combine with the shallots, salt, and pepper. Stir gently with a large spoon, mixing in the heavy cream. Continue stirring just to incorporate the cream. Taste and reseason if needed. Transfer the mixture to a plastic pastry bag (see sidebar below) and cut off about ½-inch of the tip of the bag. Set aside.

Then start the sauce. Pour the juice into a medium stainless steel saucepan over high heat, bring up to a boil, reduce the heat to medium, and simmer gently until the juice has reduced to a sauce-like consistency, leaving about 1½ cups. Pour the sauce into a small bowl and chill.

To roast the beets, preheat the oven to 350°F. Place the beets in a large roasting pan. Drizzle the beets with olive oil and toss to coat. Pour in the orange juice, cover with aluminum foil, and bake until cooked through, 1 to 1½ hours, depending on the size of the beets. Once the beets are cooked, remove the foil and allow the beets to cool enough to be handled. To peel while still keeping the top intact, gently squeeze the beet at its root end and pull off the skin.

At the restaurant, Weaver uses narrow white rectangular plates for a dramatic presentation, but use whatever you have available along with your creativity to assemble the dish. For each serving, squeeze a ½-inch-wide, 4-inch-long band of the goat cheese mixture onto the plate. Next, arrange 5 beets (halve them if they are larger) equidistant from one another on each plate, nestling them gently into the goat cheese. Place a few sprigs of mâche between the beets for color. Sprinkle a bit of salt and pepper over each beet. Drizzle approximately 1 tablespoon of sauce over each beet and along the sides of the beets. Serve immediately.

INSTANT PASTRY BAG

Unless you're icing a fancy cake, you can frequently get away with simply grabbing a plastic sandwich bag. Fill the bag, snip one corner, and squeeze to pipe whatever you're working with. The plastic bag becomes an instant pastry bag, but better: Because it's disposable, you don't have to worry about cleaning it when you're through.

UNO MAS

880 ALLBRITTON BOULEVARD, MOUNT PLEASANT
(843) 856-4868
WWW.DINEWITHSAL.COM
EXECUTIVE CHEF: JOHN NATILI

A member of the prolific Mustard Seed Restaurant Group owned by restaurant baron Sal Parco, Uno Mas is equal parts Mexican and Texan/American. "If you want something simple like an enchilada or a quesadilla, you can get it, but you'll also be able to order grilled mahimahi from the specials board," says executive chef John Natili.

More than anything, the restaurant—resplendent in chunky, old-world wood and cheery south-of-the-border colors—is outright fun. Chirpy Mexican tunes handily wash away workday stress, especially when fortified with a sprightly cool margarita. Uno Mas attracts a mostly young crowd from burgeoning Mount Pleasant, a rapidly growing suburb situated just over the Arthur Ravenel Bridge and only minutes from downtown.

Mango, shrimp, and fresh lime juice flirt deliciously in Uno Mas's Guacamole Camarón (*camarón* means "shrimp" in Spanish). Since the restaurant's opening day, the guacamole here has been a runaway hit. John says its popularity lies in its freshness: "We make it the second before people are actually eating it." The avocados are cut and smashed to order in Mexican mortars made from lava rock, and served in the very same vessel for an authentic look and texture. A regular mortar and pestle will do in your kitchen, but by all means eschew using a food processor, as it will tear and bruise the avocado and spoil the guacamole.

GUACAMOLE CAMARÓN
(Serves 8)

12 medium to large shrimp, shelled
   and deveined
1 tablespoon olive oil
Pinch of salt, plus more to taste
Pinch of ancho chile powder
12 soft medium-sized Hass avocados
¼ cup fresh-squeezed lime juice
½ cup finely chopped cilantro
1 cup diced vine-ripe tomatoes
½ cup diced red onion
1 tablespoon minced garlic
2 serrano peppers, seeded and minced
½ cup diced mango
Fresh tortilla chips, for serving

Preheat the grill or broiler. Toss the shrimp with the olive oil, salt, and ancho chile powder in a medium bowl. Grill or broil shrimp for about 2 minutes on each side, until opaque in the center. When cool enough to handle, coarsely chop into chunks about the size of large, square peas. Set aside. Meanwhile, in a large mortar or bowl, smash the avocados together with the lime juice into a chunky-smooth consistency, using either a pestle or a fork. Fold in the shrimp and the remaining ingredients (except tortilla chips) with a wooden spoon. Taste and add salt as needed. Serve in large, colorful Mexican glasses with small bowls of fresh tortilla chips for dipping.

La Fourchette

432 King Street, downtown
(843) 722-6261
Owner: Perig Goulet

When he's in the house, which is most of the time, the owner of this stateside rendition of a bona fide French bistro jumps to and fro between the twelve tables like a Gallic jumping bean, his energy infusing the space via his thick, bouncy accent and first-class customer service. Originally from Brittany, France, Perig's been in the restaurant biz since he was sixteen (good luck getting him to tell you how long ago that was) and living in Charleston for more than a decade. La Fourchette (which means "fork" in French) is the first restaurant he's owned.

"This is a new version of French bistro food," says Perig. "Most French bistros in America are a little boring. I wanted something for older people, and younger people, too." Boring, La Fourchette is not. Most nights Edith Piaf's big, pretty voice provides the recorded sound, and the able kitchen staff of three recreates the menu and recipes based on Perig's life and experiences in France. Mini-bottle Grand Marnier lights and charming black-and-white photography from the City of Light cast a playful, romantic glow while bistro staples like Blanquette de Veau and Steak Frites served with a petite salad satisfy Francophile appetites with traditional fare. All sixty wine varietals offered are imported from France, and a house Bordeaux is always in stock.

Perig declined to share his recipe for Pâté de Canard Facon Goulet, which is a smooth, buttery duck pâté, because "it's a family recipe." Instead he offered his version of Coquilles St. Jacques à la Bretagne, which reflects the flavors and style of his beloved Brittany. Indeed, Perig uses butter, cream, pork, and wine imported from Brittany to prepare the dish. The scallops are fabulous for entertaining because they can be prepped in advance and broiled at the last minute; the large, flat scallop shells are impressive natural dishes.

Coquilles St. Jacques à la Bretagne
(Serves 6)

For the sauce:

2 tablespoons peanut or canola oil
½ cup (about 3) thinly sliced shallots
½ cup diced bacon
¼ cup cognac or Armagnac
½ stick (4 tablespoons) butter, plus 1 tablespoon
    to finish the sauce
5 tablespoons all-purpose flour
½ cup white wine (Perig suggests Muscadet,
    which is indigenous to Brittany)
5 tablespoons heavy cream
Salt and freshly ground black pepper to taste

For the scallops:

1 tablespoon peanut or canola oil
2 tablespoons butter
18 large fresh sea scallops
Salt and freshly ground black pepper to taste

Special equipment: six coquille half-shells
    (available at most gourmet/specialty shops)
    or a shallow gratin dish

To prepare the sauce, heat the oil in a medium sauté pan over medium-high heat. Add the shallots and the bacon and cook, stirring, until the shallots are caramelized and the bacon is golden at the edges. Remove the pan from the heat and deglaze with cognac or Armagnac, stirring to pick up any brown bits. Return pan to high heat and reduce until the liquor has evaporated, about 2 minutes. Reduce the heat to medium and add 4 tablespoons butter. When melted, stir in the flour with a wooden spoon. Cook for 45 seconds. Add the white wine and reduce by half. Add the cream and the remaining 1 tablespoon butter. Season to taste with salt and pepper.

Meanwhile, heat the oil and butter in a large skillet over medium-high heat. Season the scallops lightly with salt and pepper. Once the oil and butter are sizzling, arrange the scallops in a single layer in the pan. Sear for about 2 minutes on one side, then flip scallops and repeat on the second side. Turn off the heat.

Remove the scallops from the pan and arrange three in each of the six half-shells (or arrange a single layer in the gratin dish). Top the scallops with sauce (about 3 tablespoons for each shell or all of it for a gratin dish). The scallops can be prepared up to this point and refrigerated overnight before broiling.

To serve, preheat broiler. Arrange the filled shells on a baking sheet, open side up. Broil on the highest oven rack until golden and bubbly, about 4 minutes. Serve immediately.

CRAVE KITCHEN AND COCKTAILS

1968 RIVIERA DRIVE, UNIT O, MOUNT PLEASANT
(843) 884-1177
WWW.CRAVEMTP.COM
OWNERS: CHRIS AND CARA DOLAN
EXECUTIVE CHEF: LANDEN GANSTROM

Upon landing at New York's LaGuardia Airport on a return trip from their Charleston-based wedding, freshly minted marital team Chris and Cara Dolan decided to quit their New York restaurant/bar management jobs and move to the Holy City. Once here, however, it was a favorite New York restaurant in a residential neighborhood at 88th Street and 3rd Avenue that inspired what would eventually become Crave's cosmopolitan menu and theme. "We tried to make a very easy lunch and dinner menu that would appeal to everyone with a little bit of everything—seafood, steaks, burgers, turkey clubs—the whole gamut," says Chris.

Crave draws raves from residents of suburban Mount Pleasant neighborhoods looking for a downtown-style meal without having to make the twenty-five-minute drive or pay Charleston's higher prices. The formula and the location work, but it's the Dolans' unwavering allegiance to customer service and executive chef Landen Ganstrom's extreme culinary talent, mixed into every bite of his ambitious thirty-plus-item menu, that make Crave stand out. From Panko-Crusted Brie Bites with a Spicy Marmalade to Pan-Seared Sea Bass with Sweet and Spicy Chili Ginger Glaze, happening Crave really does have it all. Even things as mundane as hummus and tapenade are transformed into magnificence with Landen's deft touch.

CREAMY GARLIC HUMMUS AND MEDITERRANEAN OLIVE TAPENADE
(Makes 8 to 10 appetizer portions)

For hummus:

2½ (15.5-ounce) cans garbanzo beans
¾ cup tahini paste
⅓ cup fresh-squeezed lemon juice
5 cloves garlic
½ teaspoon salt
1 teaspoon corn syrup
1 teaspoon granulated sugar
½ cup extra-virgin olive oil
2 tablespoons toasted pine nuts, for garnish

For the tapenade:

2 cups kalamata olives
5 anchovy fillets

3 tablespoons grated Parmesan cheese
1 tablespoon extra-virgin olive oil
1 cup Spanish queen stuffed olives
½ teaspoon freshly ground black pepper
3 cloves roasted garlic (see roasting garlic, page 97)
¼ cup diced red bell pepper
¼ cup diced yellow bell pepper

For serving:

Fresh baby greens
Flatbread or pita points
Fruity olive oil (optional)

To prepare the hummus, combine all of the ingredients except the olive oil and pine nuts in the bowl of a food processor. Pulse until very smooth. Remove from food processor and put into a bowl. Gradually incorporate the olive oil in a slow drizzle. Taste and adjust seasoning as needed.

To prepare the tapenade, combine all of the ingredients except the bell peppers in the bowl of a food processor. Pulse until blended and coarsely minced. Remove the mixture from the food processor and spoon into a medium-sized bowl. Fold in the diced bell peppers. Taste and adjust seasoning as needed.

This dish can be served on a platter or on individual plate. For either, place the desired amount of hummus and tapenade (about 4 tablespoons of each for a single serving) on either side of a pretty plate. Drizzle with fresh baby greens and serve with flatbread or toasted pita points. Drizzle with a fruity olive oil if desired and scatter some of the pine nuts over the hummus. Serve both at room temperature.

Samos Taverna

819 Coleman Boulevard, Mount Pleasant
(843) 856-5055
Owner/Partner: George Malanos
Executive Chef: Phil Wallace

Let's face it. Greek food generally doesn't get the respect it deserves. For the longest time, most Greek offerings in Charleston were muddled—certainly not Olympian. Then along came Samos.

Open since early 2009, Samos sparkles like the Greek island for which it is named, a brilliant atoll lapped by Greek menu goodness and dappled with 100 percent Greek familial love. Retired M.D. and first-generation American George Malanos thought Charleston needed a good Greek restaurant, so he built it on memories of a lifetime of visits to his father's birthplace, a village (population 180) on the island of Samos.

George and his wife spent six months in the kitchen with executive chef Phil Wallace tasting and tweaking dishes like the swoon-worthy moussaka, deliciously dusted with cinnamon, and plump orzo, redolent with fresh herbs, to perfection. Phil's "modern Greek cuisine" is just that, but the sincere flavors and heart of the place speak to a deep respect for the traditions of the old country. The soothing, sophisticated decor is miles away from cliché, instead showcasing gorgeous black-and-white photographs of family members taken by family members, dramatic, chunky retro lights, accommodating chocolate leather booths, and more candles and pillows than you can count.

Melitzano salata is a brightly flavored eggplant dip that glitters with lemon and cilantro. It will surely bring a bit of Samos to your kitchen. Chef Wallace and his tasting team adapted this, and several other dishes at the restaurant, from the cookbook *The Real Greek at Home: Dishes from the Heart of the Greek Kitchen* by Theodore Kyriakou and Charles Campion.

Melitzano Salata
(Makes 4 to 6 appetizer portions)

1 medium eggplant
2 tablespoons olive oil
⅓ cup walnuts
¼ cup finely chopped fresh cilantro
½ cup thinly sliced scallions
1 small shallot, finely diced
2 teaspoons finely minced garlic
1 tablespoon fresh-squeezed lemon juice
Salt and freshly ground black pepper to taste

Cut eggplant in half lengthwise. Score the flesh in a crisscross pattern with a knife. Rub 1 tablespoon olive oil generously over the cut surfaces and grill on a hot grill (or under the broiler), turning several times, until soft, 12 to 15 minutes. Remove eggplant from the oven and cool to room temperature. Scoop out the flesh and chop into ¼-inch chunks.

After the eggplant has cooked, turn off broiler and preheat oven to 350°F. Roast the walnuts in a roasting pan for 8 minutes, or until golden. Remove from the oven and coarsely chop into chunks about the same size as the eggplant chunks. Combine the eggplant and the walnuts with the remaining ingredients. Taste and adjust seasoning as needed. Serve at room temperature, individually or on a platter with an ample basket of warmed pita wedges. The dip can be prepared a day or two in advance and stored in an airtight container in the refrigerator.

J. Paul'z

1739 Maybank Highway, Suite V, James Island
(843) 795-6995
www.jpaulz.com
Executive Chef: Daniel Caruso

Chatting with a James Islander about being a James Islander is somewhat akin to chatting with a New York Yankees fan about being a New York Yankees fan. James Islanders are fervently and fanatically proud of their island, situated on the other side of the Ashley River and the harbor from peninsular Charleston. Known for its family-friendliness, middle-class values, and attachment to Folly Beach ("The Edge of America") at the far tip of the island, James Island's gourmet résumé has traditionally been abbreviated.

Executive chef Daniel Caruso fattened it up big time when he took the reins at J. Paul'z, a small-plate gold mine that rightly took James Island and Charleston by storm when a huge tapas wave rolled in in 2005. J. Paul'z debuted with a Spanish theme (witness the huge bull paintings that still flank the front door), but Daniel has since infused his seasonally revolving menu with an alluring combination of Asian and new American influences—also including a delightfully unexpected bedfellow: made-to-order sushi.

The restaurant has developed a loyal following of revelers in search of first-class food and a good time at a reasonable price. The gleeful, boldly colorful velvet cushions, divider curtains, and sand and sea-glass filled tables add to the relaxed sense of sophistication at J. Paul'z.

Though Daniel regularly changes the menu, he says Crispy Red Snapper is always on the menu—"or customers will get mad." The remarkable dish showcases mild fish caught in local waters, served over forbidden rice, a black, chewy, almost seedlike joy that counters the mildness of the fish and the bite of the soy lime reduction to a T. Look for forbidden rice online or in Chinese specialty shops.

Crispy Red Snapper over Forbidden Black Rice with Shiitake Mushrooms and Asparagus and a Soy-Lime Reduction

(Serves 4)

For the rice:

1 tablespoon butter
1 small yellow onion, diced
½ pound (about 1¼ cups) forbidden black rice
1½ cups white wine
8 cups chicken stock
Salt to taste

For the sauce:

Reserved stems from shiitake mushrooms
   (see below)
2 cups sliced shallots
4 tablespoons honey
1 cup soy sauce
1 cup fresh-squeezed lime juice
2 cups chicken stock
3 tablespoons butter
Salt and freshly ground black pepper to taste

For the fish and vegetable garnish:

4 4-ounce fresh red snapper fillets
Salt and freshly ground black pepper to taste
1 tablespoon butter
1 cup 1-inch pieces fresh asparagus
20 shiitake mushrooms caps, sliced
1 tablespoon olive oil

To prepare the rice, melt the butter over medium heat in a 4-quart saucepan. Add the onion and sauté until translucent and tender, about 5 minutes. Add the rice, tossing to coat with butter. Toast the rice for a few minutes, until it releases a nutty aroma. Increase the heat to high, add the white wine, and reduce until almost dry. Add the chicken stock and salt. Bring rice to a boil, then reduce to a simmer and cover. Cook until the rice has absorbed all of the liquid and is tender, about 45 minutes to 1 hour.

To prepare the sauce, begin by pulling the "feet" off the shiitake mushrooms that will garnish the fish. Slice them thinly and set aside. Sauté the shallots and the shiitake stems together over medium heat in a medium-sized saucepan with 1 tablespoon butter until just softened, about 2 minutes. Add the honey, stir, and continue to cook until the onions and mushrooms soften and take on a golden caramel color. Add the soy sauce, lime juice, and chicken stock, then increase the heat to high. Continue cooking until the liquid is reduced by half. Strain the sauce through a fine sieve or chinois and return to the pan until ready to serve.

Rinse and pat the fish dry with paper towels. Season both sides generously with salt and pepper. Heat the butter in a large sauté pan over medium-high heat. Place the fish in the pan in a single layer and cook for about 3 minutes. Delicately turn the fish using a flat spatula and repeat on the second side. You're shooting for a golden crust and barely opaque, milky center. Remove the fish from the pan and set aside.

Using the same pan, add 1 tablespoon olive oil and sauté the asparagus and sliced mushroom caps over medium-high heat, tossing and seasoning to taste, for about 3 minutes.

To serve, heat the sauce if needed, taste, and adjust seasoning. Whisk in 3 tablespoons of butter. Divide the rice among four plates and top with a fillet of fish. Surround the fish with the sautéed vegetables and dress the entire plate with a generous amount (2 ounces or so) of sauce. Serve immediately.

Peninsula Grill

112 North Market Street, downtown
(843) 723-0700
www.peninsulagrill.com
Partner/Executive Chef: Robert Carter

Peninsula Grill feels a bit like a Southern gentlemen's club that wisely and graciously invites the ladies, on bent knee, to supper and later into the parlor (that is, bar) for a dandy of a mint julep and some romantic banter. Suave, swank, and debonair, Peninsula Grill is decorated with restrained Southern taste and hushed by soothing, slate-gray, velvet-lined walls and nineteenth-century portraits of celebrated Charlestonians. Intimate, with just one hundred seats in the dining area, Peninsula Grill is Charleston's premier special occasion restaurant and one of her most revered. People come from near and far on birthdays, anniversaries, and other notable life occasions for Robert Carter's elegant (but never prissy) new American cuisine with Southern influences.

Robert's been steering the ship here since the restaurant opened in 1997, garnering awards and international praise along the way. Though many menus have been modified over the years, he still sticks to the original plan—"a timeless restaurant that is identifiable as both upscale and casual." Toward that end, he gives diners "steakhouse" choices, like simple grilled steak and seafood paired with a number of sauces (ponder toasted pecan–rosemary butter sauce for a fleeting indulgence!), and dishes he constructs, like his signature Seared Foie Gras with Black Pepper–Duck Biscuits and Carolina Peach Jam. For the essence of Robert's gutsy, boyish Southern style, ask why the dish is such a hit; he says with a humble smile, "It works." Duck confit, essentially duck slowly braised in duck fat (the duck must be entirely covered by the fat), is the principal layer of the dish. "It is a great staple to have in your refrigerator for all kinds of last-minute entertaining, so double or triple the recipe when you make it," advises Robert. Confit will store well, refrigerated, for one or two months.

Seared Foie Gras with Black Pepper–Duck Biscuits and Carolina Peach Jam
(Serves 6)

For the duck confit:

2 duck legs
1 tablespoon kosher salt
1 bay leaf
1 teaspoon whole black peppercorns
3 sprigs fresh thyme
3 cups duck fat (available online or at specialty stores)

Special equipment: **an ovenproof crock, Dutch oven, or heavy enameled frying pan large enough to hold the duck legs and the fat**

For the peach jam:

½ pound ripe peaches (about 3 peaches), peeled and sliced
1½ cups granulated sugar
3 tablespoons water
¼ cup brandy

For the biscuits:

1 cup self-rising flour (Robert suggests White Lily
  brand, a Southern flour milled from soft, low-
  protein wheat)
Pinch of salt
1½ teaspoons freshly ground black pepper
2 tablespoons cold unsalted butter, cubed
⅓–½ cup milk (depending on the protein content
  of the flour; Robert says to "practice, practice,
  practice" to get the ratio right)

For the foie gras:

1¼–1½ pounds whole foie gras, cut into 3½-ounce
  pieces

Special equipment: a large ovenproof,
  heavy-bottomed sauté pan

To garnish the plates:

A few tablespoons good-quality French
  whole-grain mustard
2 cups fresh petite-leaf lettuce

To prepare the duck confit, toss the duck legs, salt, bay leaf, peppercorns, and thyme in a bowl. Transfer to a gallon ziplock bag and refrigerate overnight. The next day, preheat the oven to 275°F. Melt the duck fat in the ovenproof crock or frying pan on the stove over medium heat. Remove the duck legs from the ziplock bag and wipe off with a paper towel. Place the duck legs in the crock or frying pan, immersing completely in the duck fat. Cover tightly with lid or foil, place in the oven, and bake for 4 to 6 hours, or until the duck is falling off the bone. Remove from the oven and cool for 30 minutes. If using immediately, remove the duck from the fat, remove and discard the skin, and pull the flesh off the bone. Shred the duck meat and set aside. (To store duck confit longer, leave the whole duck legs in the fat, cover tightly, and refrigerate for up to 3 months.) You will need ½ cup of shredded duck to make 6 servings of the biscuits.

To prepare the peach jam, puree the peaches until they are smooth. Place the peach puree and remaining ingredients in a heavy-bottomed nonreactive saucepan. Bring to a simmer over low heat and simmer, stirring occasionally, for about 30 minutes, or until thickened to jam consistency. Skim the top as needed to remove any foam. Set aside. (The jam can be made several days in advance and refrigerated in a sealed container until ready to use. Warm the jam to room temperature before serving.)

To prepare the black pepper biscuits, preheat the oven to 500°F. In a large bowl, combine the flour, salt, and pepper. Add the butter and, using two knives or a pastry cutter, quickly cut in the butter until it is in pieces the size of small peas. With a fork, blend in the milk until the dough comes away from the sides of the bowl. The inside of the dough should still be wet to the touch. (Be careful not to overwork the dough, or the biscuits will be tough.) Lightly flour a pastry board. Put the dough on it and pat it together, gently, into a ¾-inch-thick round. Using a 2-inch round biscuit cutter, cut out 6 biscuits. Place on an ungreased baking sheet and bake for 6 to 8 minutes, or until golden. Allow to cool slightly. (The biscuits can be made 1 day ahead, cooled, and stored in an airtight container, but are best fresh out of the oven.)

To prepare the foie gras, preheat the oven to 450°F. Heat the ovenproof sauté pan over medium-high heat on the stove until it is sizzling hot. Place the foie gras slices in the pan and sear until golden, about 1 minute on each side. Place the pan in the hot oven for 3 minutes. Turn the pieces of foie gras over and return the pan to the oven for 1 minute more. The foie gras should be golden brown and spring back to a gentle touch.

To serve, cut the biscuits in half horizontally and spread the bottoms lightly with French whole-grain mustard. Fill each with a few tablespoons of the prepared pork and top with the biscuit top. Place a slice of foie gras on each plate, one filled biscuit-sandwich off to the side, and a dollop (about 2 tablespoons) of the peach jam off to the side. Garnish with a sprinkling of petite-leaf lettuce.

THE BOATHOUSE RESTAURANTS

THE BOATHOUSE ON ELLIS CREEK
1241 HARBOR VIEW ROAD, JAMES ISLAND
(843) 577-7171
EXECUTIVE CHEF: CHARLES ARENA

THE BOATHOUSE AT BREACH INLET
101 PALM BOULEVARD, ISLE OF PALMS
(843) 886-8000
WWW.BOATHOUSERESTAURANTS.COM
EXECUTIVE CHEF: BRANNON FLORIE

Born and raised in Brooklyn, New York, toting a Sicilian lineage, and bald-headed, Charles Arena, executive chef of The Boathouse on Ellis Creek, looks like a tough guy. In fact, he's a softie, especially when it comes to his love for fresh, local, and sustainable fish. "If you're cooking fresh fish right and seasoning it right, in most cases you just need to brush a little butter on top and you're good to go. There is no use masking the flavor," says Charles.

After years of cultivating relationships with local fishermen when he was chef at sister restaurant The Boathouse at Breach Inlet (now the domain of executive chef Brannon Florie), Arena has amassed an armada of contacts who ensure that only the freshest local finds show up at his kitchen door every morning. "We always try to have local grouper and triggerfish and, when in season, stock local swordfish, local snapper, and local mahimahi," explains Charles. Somehow, the restaurant's view of waving marsh and sparkling blue waters makes Charles's gorgeous fish dishes taste and look even fresher.

The following recipe is a favorite at the restaurants. Once you try it, you'll understand why. The extra good news is that the fritters are surprisingly easy to make.

CRAB FRITTERS WITH
MILD GREEN TABASCO CREAM SAUCE
(Makes about 24 fritters or 6 servings)

For the fritters:

1 cup Duke's Mayonnaise
1 teaspoon Old Bay Seasoning
Juice of ½ lemon
1 tablespoon dried parsley
1 egg
Salt and freshly ground black pepper to taste

¼ pound lump crabmeat
¼ pound jumbo lump crabmeat
¼ pound crab claw meat
1 cup panko bread crumbs plus ½ cup for coating
4 tablespoons canola or vegetable oil

For the cream sauce:

Juice of 1 lemon
2 cups white wine
3 tablespoons rice wine vinegar
1 shallot, minced
1 5-ounce bottle Tabasco Green Pepper Sauce
1 quart (4 cups) heavy cream
3 tablespoons cornstarch
Salt and freshly ground black pepper to taste

For garnish:

Fresh parsley, chopped

Begin by prepping the fritters. In a large bowl, combine the mayonnaise, Old Bay Seasoning, lemon juice, dried parsley, egg, salt, and pepper, whisking until smooth. Thoroughly pick over the crabmeat and remove any shells or hard shards. Add all crabmeat to the mayonnaise mixture and fold in with a wooden spoon, stirring to combine. Stir in 1 cup of the panko bread crumbs until evenly combined. Refrigerate for 30 minutes to set the fritter mixture.

Meanwhile, prepare the cream sauce. Combine the lemon juice, white wine, rice wine vinegar, and shallot in a medium saucepan. Bring to a boil over high heat. Reduce by half, or until about 1 cup of liquid remains. Add the Tabasco and cream, bring to a boil, and reduce to a simmer. In a small bowl, combine the cornstarch with enough cool water (roughly 3 to 4 tablespoons) to liquefy it, forming a slurry. Stir until a smooth, loose paste forms. Add the paste to the sauce, whisking to combine. Simmer the sauce gently until it is thick enough to coat the back of a spoon, about 10 minutes. Season to taste with salt and pepper.

Next, shape and cook the fritters. Using your hands or a small scoop, shape the cooled fritter mixture into 1-ounce balls. You should be able to make about 24. Place the reserved ½ cup panko bread crumbs in a small bowl. Roll each of the fritters gently in the crumbs to coat evenly. Heat the oil in a cast-iron pan or heavy-bottomed frying pan over medium heat. When sizzling, arrange the fritters in a single layer in the pan and fry until golden brown, about 3 minutes. You may need to work in batches. Turn each fritter and fry on the other side. Remove fritters from the pan with a slotted spoon and drain on paper towels. Season lightly with salt and pepper.

To serve, spoon about ¼ cup of the sauce on each of six plates, spreading to form a pool. Top with 4 fritters and garnish with chopped parsley. Serve immediately.

PUT UP YOUR DUKE'S!

No self-respecting Southern chef, home cook or otherwise, would settle for anything less than Duke's Mayonnaise in his or her condiment pantry. When I first moved to South Carolina, a Charleston-raised pal shrieked upon seeing Hellmann's in my refrigerator. Duke's roots go back to Greenville, South Carolina (about a four-hour drive northwest of Charleston), where it was created by Eugenia Duke in 1917. Duke's was raised in the South and its ingredient list does not contain sugar, giving it a flavor tang unlike that of many other commercial brands. Duke's, it could (and will) be heatedly argued, can only be bested by homemade mayonnaise.

CHAI'S LOUNGE & TAPAS

462 KING STREET, DOWNTOWN
(843) 722-7313
WWW.BASILTHAIRESTAURANT.COM
OWNERS: HENRY AND CHAI EANG
CHEF: DEREK FALTA

Chai's wasn't part of the original business plan for Cambodian refugees and restaurateur brothers Henry and Chai Eang, but success always has been. After years of dabbling in the restaurant business, including working in their parents' noodle house in Cambodia, the brothers Eang achieved huge success when they opened their first Thai wonder, Basil (see page 54), in 2002. In the early days, Thai-starved crowds lined up for Basil's fare often traveled to a bar across the street to have a drink while waiting to be seated. When a restaurant space opened up next door to Basil, the Eangs decided to buy it and transform it into a fusion tapas bar and lounge so they could tap into the burgeoning tapas market while simultaneously finding profitable lodging for Basil's temporarily misplaced patient fans. So Chai's was born. It bears Chai's name because he likes the late-night lounge scene, but both Henry and Chai, several local chefs, and long-standing chef Derek Falta put their professional two cents into Chai's 100 percent golden menu.

A mural of the world's largest temple, Angkor Wat, sets a dramatic stage for Chai's international menu, with Cambodian, Japanese, European, and American influences. Live music pumps up the crowd on the spacious outdoor patio in balmy weather, and most of the guests linger for the fabulous food long after drinks have been served. These burgers fly off the griddle at Chai's, where they're affectionately known as "sliders."

HANDMADE MINI ANGUS BURGERS
(Makes 16 mini burgers)

3 large sweet white onions, thinly sliced
½ stick (4 tablespoons) unsalted butter
Salt and freshly ground black pepper to taste
1 pound ground Angus beef, 20% lean

16 soft white mini burger buns (available at most grocery stores)
Pickles, mustard, and ketchup to garnish

Heat a large skillet over medium-high heat. Add the onions and butter, stir to coat, and season lightly with salt and pepper. Reduce heat to medium. Cook until the onions have softened and caramelized, about 20 minutes. Set aside to cool. Puree the onions in a food processor until chunky-smooth. In a large bowl, combine the onions with the beef and season with salt and pepper. Form the beef into 1-ounce patties.

To cook, preheat a grill or a large sauté pan over medium-high heat. Cook burgers on one side for 2 minutes and flip, repeating on the second side. Cook to medium (an internal temperature of about 155–160°F). Place each patty on a half bun and top with pickles, ketchup, and mustard. Replace the bun tops and serve.

Langdon's Restaurant and Wine Bar

778 South Shellmore Boulevard, Mount Pleasant
(843) 388-9200
WWW.LANGDONSRESTAURANT.COM
Chef-Owner: Patrick Langdon Owens

Patrick Owens's path to restaurant success was less than conventional. It included high school football, multiple road trips playing guitar with a band called No Wake, and a degree in marketing from Clemson University. What it did not include was formal culinary training. That proved to be no matter for the restaurant maverick and Mount Pleasant native, who cut his cooking baby teeth at numerous restaurants (some of them less than glamorous, including a fondue joint) before opening Langdon's in 2003. A smashing success since day one, Langdon's is a surprise treat tucked into a strip mall and has garnered five AAA Four Diamond ratings and the adoration of foodies. A bona fide white linen restaurant with a neat black and white color scheme whipped up by the young chef, Langdon's is a cosmopolitan culinary enclave of Patrick's own talented making. He wows fans with his largely Asian and clean-lined inspirations such as Pork Chops with Hoisin and Honey Glaze and Asparagus Risotto with Sautéed Jumbo Lump Crab Meat and Meyer Lemon. "I like to find what looks really good and try to put it together without it being too far out there," he says. These spring rolls are the restaurant's number-one seller, followed by Langdon's signature Short Rib Osso Bucco.

Patrick says, "If you're going to go to the trouble of making these, make it a big batch." The rolls can be prepared ahead and frozen for a month or two before frying and serving. The avocado cream, however, is highly perishable and needs to be prepared within an hour or two of serving.

Lobster and Avocado Spring Rolls with Asian Vegetables, Spicy Chili Sauce, and Avocado Cream
(Makes 30 spring rolls or 6 appetizer portions)

For the spring rolls:

6 tablespoons olive oil
2 red peppers, seeded and finely sliced
2 yellow peppers, seeded and finely sliced
1 large red onion, finely sliced
4 tablespoons finely minced garlic
4 tablespoons sesame oil
4 tablespoons finely chopped minced ginger
3 cups finely sliced napa cabbage
2 carrots, peeled and finely shredded

Generous dash each of soy sauce, rice wine vinegar, honey, and Sriracha (a spicy Thai condiment available in most grocery stores)
Salt and freshly ground black pepper to taste
½ cup finely chopped fresh cilantro, plus more for serving
2 tablespoons toasted sesame seeds
3 1-pound Maine lobsters
4 avocados, sliced ¼ inch thick
30 spring roll wrappers
1 egg
2 cups peanut oil for frying

For the avocado cream:

1 avocado
Juice of 1 lime
½ cup half-and-half
3 tablespoons heavy cream
Salt and freshly ground white pepper to taste

To prepare the spring rolls, begin by heating 3 tablespoons of olive oil in a large sauté pan over medium-high heat. Add the sliced red and yellow peppers and red onion to the pan, stir, and sauté until just softened, about 5 minutes. Just as the peppers are nearing completion, add 2 tablespoons each of garlic, sesame oil, and fresh ginger. Set aside the pepper mixture. Meanwhile, heat another 3 tablespoons of olive oil over medium-high heat in a large sauté pan. Sauté the cabbage until softened, 7 to 8 minutes. Drain off any excess liquid and set aside. In a large bowl, combine the pepper and onion mixture, the cabbage, and the raw carrots, soy sauce, rice wine vinegar, honey, and Sriracha. Season to taste with salt and pepper, mix thoroughly, cover, and refrigerate overnight. The following day, put the mixture in a large kitchen towel or cheesecloth and twist, over a sink, to squeeze out all excess liquid. Add the fresh cilantro and toasted sesame seeds to the mixture. Set aside.

Fill a large pot or a stockpot three-quarters full, salt generously, and bring up to a rolling boil over high heat. Add the live lobsters, cover, and cook for 2 minutes. Then shock the lobsters by placing them in a deep ice water bath until they are cold. Crack the lobster claws and tails, remove the meat, and coarsely chop. (The flesh will be "quite rare," according to Patrick.) Combine the lobster in a medium bowl with the remaining 2 tablespoons each of garlic, sesame oil, and fresh ginger.

To begin "spring roll perfection" (as Patrick describes these little gems), place 1 tablespoon of the vegetable mixture in the center of each spring roll wrapper. Top each with a couple chunks of lobster and a slice of avocado. (You'll want to slice the avocados just before assembling the rolls, or they will discolor.) Roll the wrappers into tight, cigarlike packages, tucking the ends into the roll to seal. Beat the egg in a small bowl and brush the top of each roll with a thin layer of egg wash. Line the rolls up in a single layer on a cookie sheet and refrigerate until ready to fry.

To prepare the avocado cream, puree the avocado, lime juice, and half-and-half in the bowl of a food processor until smooth. Slowly stream in the heavy cream through the mouth of the processor bowl while the motor is running. Season with salt and white pepper to taste and strain by pressing the mixture through a fine-mesh strainer. Set aside.

To fry the spring rolls, heat the peanut oil in a deep skillet over medium-high heat. When it has reached 350°F, add the spring rolls in batches (do not crowd!) and fry until they are golden brown and floating to the top of the skillet. Serve 5 rolls per plate, topping with a generous dollop of the avocado cream, a drizzle of Sriracha, and some sprigs of fresh cilantro.

MED-BISTRO

90 FOLLY ROAD, SOUTH WINDERMERE PLAZA, WEST ASHLEY
(843) 766-0323
WWW.THEMEDBISTRO.COM
OWNERS: REBECCA AND BUZZY NEWTON
CHEF DE CUISINE: WILL MILLER

There has been a dining establishment at this location for half a century. What was then named Zin's Deli is now known as Med-Bistro, but really only the name and some menu items have changed for as long as anyone can remember. Above all, Med-Bistro is a neighborhood lunch and dinner hot spot; owners Rebecca and Buzzy Newton of Piggly Wiggly grocery store fame refer to the place as "a deli by day and a bistro by night."

No matter the hour, guests can count on the gutsy, stick-to-your-ribs fare of burly, red-bearded chef de cuisine Will Miller, who maintains a straightforward menu of Mediterranean and Southern-inspired dishes like Calamari Tossed with Serrano Ham, Corn, Greens, and Garlic Aioli and a mean bowl of Black Bean Soup. The serenity of high-backed black leather booths is balanced by the levity of strings of tiny white lights and paper-lined tables topped with glasses of crayons that beckon kids of all ages to come out and play.

The House Chips with Blue Cheese Fondue give new meaning to the expression "no one can eat just one." A heady, chunky blue cheese sauce tops a heaping plate of flash-fried Nathan's potato chips, creating a dish that would render even the most stringent calorie counter absolutely powerless. Go for it! Life is too short to miss this indulgence.

HOUSE CHIPS WITH BLUE CHEESE FONDUE
(Serves 4)

For the fondue:

1½ cups good-quality mild blue cheese or Gorgonzola
1–1½ cups heavy cream depending on desired consistency
Light salt and freshly ground black pepper to taste

For the chips:

4 cups peanut oil
4 cups Nathan's potato chips (or another thick high-quality brand)
Salt to taste

To make the fondue, heat a medium-sized sauté pan over medium-high heat. Crumble the cheese and place it in the pan. As it begins to melt, add the cream. Simmer over medium-high heat until the sauce thickens and reduces by about one-quarter. Season with salt and pepper to taste, but be careful with the salt, as the chips and cheese are both already salty.

Meanwhile, heat the oil in a medium-sized saucepan over medium-high heat. When the temperature reaches 350°F (use a metal thermometer to gauge the temperature), add the chips all at once. Fry until golden and floating to the top, just a few minutes, 1 to 2. Remove with a slotted spoon and drain briefly on paper towels. Sprinkle the hot chips lightly with kosher salt. To serve, place a handful of chips in each of four shallow bowls and drizzle generously with the sauce. Serve hot!

SOCIAL RESTAURANT & WINE BAR

188 EAST BAY STREET, DOWNTOWN
(843) 577-5665
WWW.SOCIALWINEBAR.COM
OWNER: BRAD BALL
EXECUTIVE CHEF: DANIEL DOYLE

Rife with more than 400 wine choices, whimsical gourmet small plates, and a happening late-night scene, Social proves itself way beyond acceptable to discerning diners in search of a good time. Brad drives the wine program with a deep-seated passion for and knowledge of the stuff. He has a diploma from the Wine & Spirit Education Trust and a penchant for artisanal wines, which he buys from an exclusive band of hand-selected importers.

What to pair with that wine? Daniel's creative dinner delights, of course. The chef and his staff can be viewed through a large window near a corner of the predominantly black casual-chic dining room, as they artfully scatter culinary pixie dust on an array of stand-out dishes.

A fifty-tap Cruvinet system ensures a free and fast flow of wine to satiate the thirst of the boisterous late-night crowd that starts drifting in sometime after ten. Seekers of a quieter dining experience may want to consider an earlier arrival.

These risotto balls are reflective of Daniel's uncanny talent for contrasting flavors and textures while incorporating a genuine sense of fun into any dish. You'll love the way the crunch of the exterior yields to a chewy risotto center, spot-on delicious with the tangy bite of tomato jam. It's like biting into a gourmet Tater Tot dipped in grown-up ketchup. Brad says this is one of Social's most popular dishes and that the risotto balls are "easy, delicious, and hold up well over a period of time."

TRUFFLED RISOTTO BALLS WITH TOMATO JAM
(Makes 20–25 risotto balls or 4–5 servings)

For the tomato jam:

1 16-ounce can of diced tomatoes
¼ of a cinnamon stick
1 tablespoon granulated sugar
Shake of nutmeg
Shake of allspice
Salt and freshly ground black pepper to taste

For the risotto balls:

1 tablespoon butter
1 small white onion, diced
½ cup white wine
2 cups Arborio rice
6 cups warm chicken stock
¼ cup grated Parmesan cheese
Truffle oil to taste
Salt and freshly black ground pepper to taste
¼ cup panko bread crumbs
3 cups vegetable oil

To make the tomato jam, combine all of the jam ingredients in a large saucepan and cook over low heat until nearly all the moisture has evaporated, about 1 hour. Allow the jam to cool, then puree until smooth in either a blender or food processor. Taste the jam and adjust the seasonings as needed. Set aside. (The jam can be prepared in advance, stored for up to 3 days, and reheated before serving.)

To make the risotto balls, heat the butter in a medium saucepan over medium heat. Add the onion and cook until soft and translucent, about 4 minutes. Increase the heat to high and deglaze the pan with the white wine. Cook until the wine is completely reduced. Add the Arborio rice, stirring constantly. Add about ½ cup of the warm stock and stir. (The trick with Arborio rice is stirring, patience, and warm stock. Together these elements will yield the moist, starchy, plump rice Arborio is intended to be!) Cook the first ½ cup of stock down until the pan is almost dry and continue adding the stock in ¼ cup increments, stirring, until all the stock is gone, 20 to 25 minutes. The rice should be plump and slightly al dente. Remove the pan from the heat. Stir in the Parmesan cheese, truffle oil, and salt and pepper to taste. Spread the risotto in a thin layer on a sheet pan and refrigerate to cool. (This can be done 2 to 3 days in advance and the risotto stored, covered and refrigerated.)

To assemble the dish, reheat the jam over low heat. Preheat the oil over medium heat in a large saucepan, until it reaches 350°F. Meanwhile, roll the prepared risotto between your palms to form balls about the size of small softballs. Place the panko bread crumbs in a bowl and roll each risotto ball in the crumbs. Fry the balls in the hot oil, in batches, until they're golden brown and have risen to the top of the pan. Drain on paper towels and season lightly with salt and pepper. To serve, arrange 4 or 5 balls on a pretty plate (Daniel uses long white porcelain plates) on a bed of warm tomato jam.

Coast Bar & Grill

39-D John Street, downtown
(843) 722-8833
WWW.COASTBARANDGRILL.COM
Executive Chef: David Pell

Think Key West or Cuba, throw in a custom-made hickory and oak wood-burning grill, award-winning mojitos, and a global menu, and you've arrived at Coast, Charleston's relaxed destination for all things fish and fun. The sweet, smoky scent of the grill perfumes the old brick alley that winds toward the restaurant's double brick-arched entrance, greeting guests with an appetite-inducing sense of what's to come even before they get there.

Coast excels at composing fish-focused regional dishes from all around the world—Cuba, Brazil, Asia, Spain, and Italy are all represented here—but David's formal French training (including several apprenticeships under celebrated French chef Christian Constant) is at the heart of it all. "In France, the biggest lesson I learned was the regional focus. The French are very particular about where their food and food products come from. I'm seeing more and more of that here in Charleston and at Coast," says David, who describes his food as "simply prepared with only the best ingredients."

Faux palm trees, blowfish lamps, tin-roofed banquettes, and regular live music make Coast feel especially festive, but David is dead serious about buying local and fresh fish. Grouper, snapper, wreckfish, triggerfish, mahimahi, and American red snapper are regularly on the menu. Coast was the first restaurant in greater Charleston to serve fish tacos when it opened in 2002; now it has many imitators, but none do it quite like Coast. Served on soft flour tortillas, the mahimahi (whose name means "strong, strong" in Hawaiian) is briefly marinated in lime juice and cilantro, grilled, and topped with a sweet fresh mango and papaya salsa, guacamole, and a pert lime slaw. To replicate the smoked grill flavor at home, Pell suggests piling the marinated fish chunks together in a metal pie plate and placing them over a gas or charcoal grill equipped with a layer of dampened hickory or mesquite wood chips.

Baja Fish Tacos
(Makes 8 tacos or 4 servings)

For the guacamole:

3 ripe avocados
Juice of 2 limes
2 jalapeños, seeded
Salt and freshly ground black pepper to taste

For the salsa:

1 ripe mango, peeled and cut into ¼-inch dice
1 ripe papaya, peeled and cut into ¼-inch dice
¼ cup finely chopped fresh mint
¼ cup finely chopped fresh parsley
½ red bell pepper, seeded and cut into ¼-inch dice
Juice of 1 orange
Juice of 2 limes
Salt and freshly ground black pepper to taste

For the lime slaw:

1 head iceberg lettuce, shredded into thin strips
Juice of 2 limes
Salt and freshly ground black pepper to taste

For the fish:

12 ounces fresh mahimahi (or substitute another
    sturdy, moist fish like tuna or grouper) cut into
    1-inch cubes (approximately 2 cups)
Juice of 2 limes
¼ cup finely chopped fresh cilantro
4–5 tablespoons extra-virgin olive oil
Salt and freshly ground black pepper to taste
8 soft flour tortillas

Special equipment: 2 cups hickory or
    mesquite chips

To prepare the guacamole, combine all of the
guacamole ingredients in the bowl of a food
processor. Blend until chunky-smooth. Taste and
adjust salt and pepper as needed. Cover with
plastic wrap and set aside at room temperature.

Next, prepare the salsa. Combine all of the salsa
ingredients in a large bowl and toss well. Taste
and adjust salt and pepper as needed.

To prepare the lime slaw, toss the lettuce, lime
juice, and salt and pepper together in a large
bowl. Season to taste. (While the guacamole and
salsa can be made a few hours in advance, the
slaw should be prepared within 20 minutes of
serving to ensure crispness.)

Preheat a gas or charcoal grill and soak a handful
of wood chips in water. Meanwhile, mix the
mahimahi with the remaining ingredients (except
the tortillas) in a bowl. Allow the fish to marinate
for 10 minutes before cooking.

To cook, stack the fish in a small pile in a pie pan
or heat-resistant container (this helps the fish
steam and stay moist), toss the wood chips on
the fire, place the pie plate pan on the grill grate,
and cover the grill. Cook about 5 minutes or until it
is firm, yet pliant to the touch and cooked through
to a faint pink center. Set fish aside briefly to rest.

To serve, quickly warm the tortillas on the grill or
in the oven, just until pliable and warm, about
2 minutes. Spread a thin layer of guacamole on the
center of each tortilla. Top with a thin layer of lime
slaw and about 1½ ounces of the cooked fish. Top
this with a generous portion of salsa. Place 2 tacos
on each plate or serve on a platter. The key is to
enjoy—immediately!—says David.

PAVILION BAR

225 EAST BAY STREET (AT THE MARKET PAVILION HOTEL), DOWNTOWN
(843) 266-4222
WWW.MARKETPAVILION.COM
EXECUTIVE CHEF: DEMETRE CASTANAS

Having cooked in a restaurant in some capacity since he was five years old, Demetre Castanas is a member of a large Greek clan that has been in the hotel and restaurant business for generations. "This is a good thing, because Greeks like to cook," Demetre says with a laugh.

Demetre oversees both kitchens at the Market Pavilion Hotel. The Pavilion Bar is a luxe rooftop hot spot with open views of the Cooper River and Charleston Harbor. The restaurant boasts sexy, sophisticated eats from Lobster Thermidor and Portobello Pizza to the decadent Duck Confit Nachos featured here.

The upscale hotel is a popular wedding reception destination. And it's likely that more than one of those weddings was conceived with a proposal at this ultraromantic, cosmopolitan spot, with sweeping waterfront vistas and an azure blue swimming pool with a gurgling waterfall.

An enforced dress code and the cosmopolitan menu ensure a steady stream of interesting people views, too. Enjoying Demetre's self-described "fun, light" fare while sipping one of the restaurant's specialty drinks (Paviliontini, anyone?) on a warm, breezy Charleston evening is tough to beat—especially if you manage to avoid falling in the swimming pool from the sheer giddiness of it all.

This recipe has it all—ooey gooey cheese, the round, earthy flavors of duck confit, the kick of peppery heat, and sweet fruit.

Duck Confit Nachos with Red Onions, Tomatoes, Pineapple Salsa, and Blue Corn Tortilla

(Serves 4)

For the duck confit:

4 duck breasts, skin-on
¼ cup coarse salt (preferably sea salt or
     kosher salt)
1 bay leaf
3 cloves garlic
3 sprigs fresh thyme
4 cups duck fat (available online or at specialty
     stores), cold or at room temperature

For the salsa:

1 cup diced fresh pineapple
½ cup diced red onion
½ cup seeded and diced red bell pepper
½ cup finely chopped fresh cilantro
Salt and freshly ground black pepper to taste

For the queso sauce:

1 stick (¼ pound) butter
¼ cup diced shallot
¼ cup seeded and diced jalapeños
¼ cup all-purpose flour
1 pint heavy cream
2 cups shredded Monterey Jack cheese
Salt and freshly ground black pepper to taste

For serving:

About 4 cups best-quality blue corn tortilla chips

Prepare the confit up to several weeks in advance
(it will store well, refrigerated) or at least 12 hours
before assembling the entire dish. Preheat the

oven to 250°F. Toss all of the confit ingredients
together in a sturdy medium roasting pan, coating
the duck breasts evenly. Arrange the duck breasts
in a single layer in the pan, cover the pan tightly
with aluminum foil, and cook for 12 to 14 hours.
Remove from the oven and allow to cool. Pull the
duck breasts apart into chunky strips with your
fingers, covering the duck with rendered fat, and
return to the pan, cover the pan, and refrigerate
to store. (You will need 1 cup of the confit for this
recipe. Save the rest for another use.)

To prepare the salsa, combine all the salsa
ingredients in a medium bowl, tossing to mix.
Taste and adjust salt and pepper as needed.
Cover and let salsa stand at room temperature
for 1 hour to develop the flavors or refrigerate
overnight. Bring the salsa to room temperature
before serving to maximize the flavor and to keep
the nachos good and hot. (This makes more salsa
than you will need. The remainder is great as a dip
for leftover chips—if there are any.)

To prepare the queso sauce, melt the butter over
medium heat and add the shallot and jalapeños.
Sauté until softened, about 3 minutes. Reduce the
heat to low. Add the flour and whisk vigorously for
about 8 minutes, or until the roux has thickened
and has no visible lumps. Increase the heat to
medium-high, add the cream, and bring to a low
simmer, whisking constantly. Once the sauce is
thickened and gently bubbling, add the cheese
and stir to melt. Add salt and pepper as needed.

The dish can be served on individual plates or on a
platter. Just before serving, reheat 1 cup of confit
in a pan over low heat. Toss the duck (discard any
excess fat) with the chips in a large bowl. Arrange
in a mound and drizzle generously with the queso
sauce. Top with a few dollops of the salsa.

FLEET LANDING

186 Concord Street, downtown
(843) 722-8100
www.fleetlanding.net
Owners: Tradd and Weesie Newton
Chef: Drew Hedlund

Housed in a former World War II U.S. Navy debarkation station, Fleet Landing maintains the unique distinction on this water-wrapped peninsula of being the only restaurant of note that actually sits on the water's edge. Unobstructed views of Charleston's picturesque harbor combined with the restaurant's casual, maritime mood and eclectic menu of Southern staples and seafood make Fleet a go-to place, especially on gorgeous sunny days or warm, breezy nights, when the restaurant's food suits the mood.

The Newtons, who caught the restaurant bug when Tradd was in charge of advertising and new store development at landmark McCrady's restaurant (see page 148), had the insight and guts to transform this long-deserted building into his dream, draping it with nautical nuances from life jackets to rope, while maintaining its original austere lines. The effect is winning and pairs well with chef Drew Hedlund's uncomplicated and well-balanced menu. A fisherman himself, Drew draws on the inspiration of local waters and local produce to create a weekly "locavore" meal, but he doesn't shy away from beefy burgers or a rib-eye topped with house-made pimiento cheese. The golf ball–sized hush puppies, stuffed with a seafood and vegetable velouté, are a house favorite. Stuffing them halfway through the cooking process can be a bit of a challenge, but it's worth the effort. The filling is a big tasty surprise in the center of these fluffy fried delights. High-quality prepared lobster and crab stocks, as well as hush puppy mix, save time and can be purchased at most grocery stores. Don't scrimp on the seafood, however—remember to buy local and fresh whenever possible!

FLEET LANDING STUFFED HUSH PUPPIES
(Makes 12 large puppies or 6 appetizer portions)

3 cups heavy cream
2½ cups water
2 cups lobster stock
1 cup crab stock
Salt and freshly ground black pepper to taste
4 sticks (1 pound) plus 2 tablespoons unsalted butter
3 ears fresh corn, shucked and kernels cut from the cobs
3 leeks (white parts only), well washed and finely julienned
3½ cups all-purpose flour
1½ teaspoons Old Bay Seasoning

Pinch of cayenne pepper
Pinch of freshly ground white pepper
¼ teaspoon ground cumin
1 1-pound box best-quality hush puppy mix (you will probably need eggs and milk, depending on the brand selected)
4 cups peanut oil
12 large (26–30 count) shrimp, peeled and deveined
2 cups fresh lobster meat
½ cup white wine
Fresh parsley, chopped (optional)

Begin by preparing the velouté sauce. In a large pot, bring the cream, water, lobster and crab stock, and salt and pepper to a low boil over high heat. In the meantime, melt 1 pound of butter in a large soup pot or stockpot over medium-high heat. Add the corn kernels and leeks to the melted butter pot, stirring, and cook over medium heat until both vegetables are just softened, about 5 minutes. Add the flour all at once, stirring to coat the vegetables evenly. Cook for about 3 minutes, and then gradually incorporate the simmering liquid mixture, stirring well to avoid lumps. Add the Old Bay Seasoning, cayenne pepper, white pepper, and cumin. Stir to incorporate, then reduce the heat to low and simmer the velouté until it is thick enough to coat the back of a spoon, about 12 minutes.

Meanwhile, prepare the hush puppy batter according to the manufacturer's directions. Heat the peanut oil to 350°F in a fryer or a deep skillet. Once the oil is hot, scoop the batter, using a large ice-cream scoop, into the oil. Fry until the hush puppies are about one quarter of the way done, about 2 minutes. Remove from the fryer and drain on paper towels. When they are cool enough to handle, cut a small piece off the bottom of each puppy with a serrated knife. This will create a steady base for the puppy to sit on. Next, cut a ¼-inch-thick slice off the top of each, and with a small fork, gently remove the raw batter in the center, leaving a sturdy ¼-inch-thick wall. Set the puppies and their tops aside.

To finish the velouté, melt the remaining 2 tablespoons of butter over medium heat in a large pot. Add the shrimp and lobster. Sauté, tossing, until the seafood is almost translucent, about 4 minutes. Deglaze the pot with the white wine and reduce until the wine forms a glaze, about 1 minute. Add the simmering vegetable velouté sauce and stir. Taste and adjust salt and pepper as needed.

Return the cored hush puppies (but not the tops) to the hot (350°F) oil and fry until completely cooked and golden, another 5 or 6 minutes. Remove with a slotted spoon and briefly drain on paper towels. Using a small soup spoon, fill each puppy with velouté and replace the reserved tops. Serve immediately, placing 2 hush puppies on each shallow plate. Garnish, if desired, with a sprinkle of fresh chopped parsley.

Salads

Between the growing season that hardly ever sleeps and the thriving South Carolina agricultural industry (topped only by tourism), fruits, vegetables, and the stuff of salads have been principal players in Charleston kitchens since colonial times. A frugal, seasonally attuned lot, Charlestonians and Charleston chefs increasingly turn to the area's many local farmers and the verdant bins of local farmers' markets for inspiration. The first blush of spring ushers in young baby lettuces, spinach, and sweet onions, followed by the plump blueberries, raspberries, and peaches of summer. With the chill of autumn arrive apples from North Carolina and the South's siren call of greens—including mustard, collard, turnip, and kale.

At FIG, chef Mike Lata's signature salad affords a wintry blend of tart radicchio slivers tossed with the sweetness of warm Lowcountry brown shrimp and a mustard vinaigrette. Two distinctly different but equally delicious versions of another beloved Charleston mainstay—chicken salad—make a splashy showing at Cru Café on Pinckney Street and the Glass Onion. Pale emerald ribbons of zucchini slither silkily in olive oil and preserved lemons at Caviar & Bananas, while smooth goat cheese meets its match with the crunch of pistachio and fancy greens at Atlanticville Restaurant and Wines on breezy, beautiful Sullivan's Island.

FIG

232 Meeting Street, downtown
(843) 805-5900
www.eatatfig.com
Chef and Partner: Mike Lata
Managing Partner: Adam Nemirow

FIG's ultratalented chef-owner Mike Lata and his partner in too-good-to-be-true culinary crime, Adam Nemirow, regularly shift their menu with changes in the Lowcountry's produce and fishing seasons, like the ebb and flow of the tide. The FIG constant? Exquisite food. Mike's entirely unfettered style speaks to the pure beauty of something as simple as a beet or a farm-fresh egg—he drizzles the former with olive oil, salt, and pepper and converts the latter into a heavenly deviled egg. Some chefs talk the local produce talk, but Mike walks the walk, along a straight line of determined devotion to the freshest of the fresh, tossed with impeccable technique and no small amount of love.

Nominated Best Chef of the Southeast by the James Beard Foundation in 2007 and 2008, he finally grabbed the prize in spring, 2009. Mike has kept this dish on FIG's menu since the restaurant's opening night in 2003. Like so many classic dishes, it was conceived out of necessity. A local farmer failed to deliver the kale Mike had initially planned to use, so he substituted the fresh radicchio he had on hand. The warm salad became an instant hit. It's best during the cooler months, when Lowcountry waters teem with sweet, milky white shrimp (see sidebar, page 49). Their incomparable briny crustacean flavors meet their match with warm, crisp, and mildly tart radicchio slivers and the salty edge of seared pancetta.

Warm Shrimp and Radicchio Salad with Pancetta and Mustard Vinaigrette

(Serves 4)

For the vinaigrette:

½ cup sherry vinegar
4 tablespoons Dijon mustard
4 shallots, minced
Salt and freshly ground black pepper to taste
1 cup plus 2 tablespoons canola oil

For the salad:

2 tablespoons olive oil
½ pound thinly sliced pancetta, julienned
1 pound white shrimp, peeled and deveined (or substitute whatever is fresh and local)

2 heads radicchio, cleaned and cut into ¼-inch-thick strips
2 bunches scallions, thinly sliced
1 pint (about 2 cups) grape tomatoes, rinsed and halved

To prepare the vinaigrette, whisk together the sherry vinegar, Dijon mustard, shallots, and salt and pepper in a medium bowl. Gradually incorporate the oil in a slow drizzle, while whisking, until emulsified. Taste and adjust salt and pepper as needed. Set aside.

To prepare the salad, heat a large sauté pan over medium heat. Add the olive oil and pancetta. Cook for 2 or 3 minutes, or until the pancetta becomes translucent. Add the shrimp and continue cooking, stirring occasionally, until the shrimp are nearly cooked through, about 4 minutes. Add the remaining salad ingredients to the pan and toss to warm through. Mike cautions against letting the radicchio get too hot, or it will wilt and become too soft (this step should only take a minute). Transfer the salad to a large bowl and toss lightly with the vinaigrette. Use just enough to lightly coat the salad; reserve any remaining vinaigrette for a later use. Season the salad lightly with salt and pepper if needed. Divide among four salad plates, carefully arranging the shrimp around the salads. Serve immediately.

LITTLE BIG SHRIMP

Shrimp are to the Lowcountry what crawfish are to Louisiana. The salt water that wraps its way around the coastal plain and weaves into the region's complex network of marshes and tributaries provides a nurturing environment for shrimp to spawn and grow before they're harvested. When that happens (generally the season runs from May or June until the first frost in December or January), shrimp of all sizes show up boiled, fried, stewed, and baked; in delicate dips, soups, salads, casseroles, deviled eggs, and omelets; and, of course, on top of grits.

Unlike shrimp "from off" (as Charlestonians refer to all things not from here), local shrimp are smaller, sweeter, and distinctive. Once you've tasted them, you'll never go back. In the warmer months, the smaller brown shrimp are running. Look for the slightly larger white shrimp, which are arguably sweeter and definitely meatier, in fall and winter.

Caviar & Bananas

51 George Street, downtown
(843) 577-7757 or toll free (877) 579-7757
www.caviarandbananas.com
Owners: Kris and Margaret Furniss
Executive Chef: Jason Ulak

When Kris Furniss decided he wanted to shift his career from finance to food, he didn't get the chance to notify his boss at Morgan Stanley. On September 11, 2001, a jet crashed into his floor at the Twin Towers, just days before he had planned to give notice. One of just 6 of 183 people on the floor to survive, Kris considers himself blessed for his miraculous survival, and he and his wife, Margaret, have found their mutual true calling in the world of gourmet food.

Their "store," a visually compelling blend of stainless steel, black and white, and shelf upon artfully stacked shelf of gourmet goodies, literally from caviar to bananas, is a friendly dine-in or take-out one-stop shop for panini, salads, sushi, wine, lattes, cookies, and any one of Jason Ulak's stellar forty-five to fifty prepared food choices that are available on any given day.

Jason refers to the case full of gorgeous food as "my life," since he's created many of the recipes over the course of his twenty-five-year professional cooking career. Mediterranean, Middle Eastern, Asian, Southern, Greek, Italian, and myriad other international flavors all make appearances here, truly following the store's motto: "Around the world in one bite." Zucchini Ribbons, a luscious salad of lemons, pecans, dried cranberries, and tender swaths of whisper-thin squash, is a favorite at Caviar & Bananas. Preserved lemons, a tart present from Moroccan cuisine, are readily available at specialty stores or can be purchased online.

Zucchini Ribbons
(Serves 4 to 6 as a side salad)

For the lemon vinaigrette:

2 preserved lemons
1 tablespoon fresh-squeezed lemon juice
1 tablespoon rice wine vinegar
1 tablespoon minced shallot
1 tablespoon Dijon mustard
2 teaspoons granulated sugar
¼ cup water
1½ cups extra-virgin olive oil

For the salad:

4 to 6 medium-sized zucchini
1½ cups candied pecans
1½ cups dried cranberries

¾ cup high-quality mild fresh goat cheese, broken into small chunks
Salt and freshly ground black pepper to taste

To prepare the lemon vinaigrette, rinse the preserved lemons very well under cool water to remove excess salt. Cut each in half, scoop out the flesh, and discard. Chop the peels finely and place in a blender or food processor with the remaining ingredients (except the olive oil). Puree until smooth. While the motor is running, gradually drizzle in the olive oil, until the vinaigrette is thick and emulsified. If the dressing is too thick, add 2 or 3 tablespoons of water. (There will be more vinaigrette than this salad recipe demands. Reserve the extra vinaigrette in a sealed container in the

refrigerator. Save it for later use as salad dressing or as a snappy sauce for fish, chicken, or vegetables.)

To assemble the salad, rinse and trim the zucchini. With a vegetable peeler, peel the zucchini from top to bottom in broad, thinly sliced strips, about the same size as ribbon candy strips, until you reach the seeds near the core. (The centers of the zucchini can be saved for soups or stuffings.) Place all the ribbons in a bowl with the remaining salad ingredients and toss well with ½ cup lemon vinaigrette to coat. Season to taste with salt and pepper. Serve immediately, piled high on attractive plates.

WHERE THE CHEFS SHOP

On Saturday mornings from early April through mid-December, chefs and Charlestonians alike bow to the region's agri-bounty at the Charleston Farmers Market. A swirl of communal energy and good times fill the air, along with the enticing aroma of made-to-order crepes and frying mini doughnuts. Spot a chef or two inspecting collards or sampling a peach. Meanwhile, peruse the booths bursting with produce, jams, pickles, crafts, dog biscuits, and more at what *Travel and Leisure* magazine deemed the fifth-best farmers' market in the entire country in 2009. The market runs from 8:00 a.m. to 2:00 p.m. on Saturdays in season and is located on Marion Square between King and Meeting Streets, downtown.

CRU CAFÉ ON PINCKNEY STREET

18 PINCKNEY STREET, DOWNTOWN
(843) 534-2434
WWW.CRUCAFE.COM
EXECUTIVE CHEF-OWNER: JOHN ZUCKER

The path to the world of food and restaurants was a winding one for John Zucker. Dreams of big-time baseball threw some curve balls in his early career, until an unlikely stint at a restaurant lead John to his culinary wake-up call at the ripe old age of twenty-seven. After researching several culinary schools, John settled on Le Cordon Bleu in Paris, where he eventually graduated first in his class and with the full blessing of his mother. "Don't waste your time over there. Get it all done and do and learn all you can," John recalls her saying.

John took her advice and wasted no time getting his latter-day culinary career on track. He was surrounded by a posse of super talents at Spago in Los Angeles, where he continued to learn as a cook, and he eventually delved into restaurant consulting in both Atlanta and Charleston. He opened Cru Café in 2001, at a time when the Thai, Hispanic, and Asian ingredients and influences he espouses were relatively foreign here. "I said, hey, we're going to educate Charleston, and we did it. We were using habañeros and poblanos, and nobody knew what they were," explains John.

With perseverance and precision, John stood true to his commitment to "staying humble and keeping it fresh" in all menu items, including his starring salad player—Chinese Chicken Salad. It's a must-try at the warm, butter-yellow, modified Charleston Single House (see sidebar, page 55) at the corner of Pinckney Street and Motley Lane. Here, the clip-clop of passing horse-drawn carriages and seasonal wafts of wisteria fill the soul with a blissful sense of all being right in the world even when, just hours earlier, it seemed all wrong.

"The key to what makes this salad so good is that when you take a bite you get everything at once—the daikon, the carrots—everything. If it's not that way, it's not getting done right," John explains.

CHINESE CHICKEN SALAD
(Serves 6 to 8)

For the roasted chicken:

1 cup garlic cloves
1 generous bunch fresh thyme, stemmed and coarsely chopped
1 tablespoon each salt and freshly ground black pepper, plus more to taste
1 large (3–4 pounds) chicken

For the dressing:

½ cup Colman's dry mustard
¾ cup peeled fresh ginger root cut into ½-inch chunks
¼ cup garlic cloves
½ cup soy sauce
¼ cup rice wine vinegar
¼ cup sesame oil
¼ cup red wine vinegar
2 cups peanut oil

¼ cup fresh-squeezed lime juice
¾ cup honey
Salt and freshly ground black pepper to taste

For the fried wontons:

3 cups peanut oil
15 prepared wonton wrappers (available at
    most grocery stores)
Salt to taste

For the salad:

3 cups julienned napa cabbage
½ cup peeled and julienned carrots
½ cup julienned daikon root
½ cup julienned red onion
½ cup julienned red bell pepper
½ cup julienned poblano peppers
Salt and freshly ground black pepper to taste

To prepare the chicken, preheat the oven to
425°F. In a bowl, mix together the garlic and the
thyme. Season the mixture with the salt and freshly
ground black pepper, blending with the garlic
and thyme. Stuff the cavity of the chicken with
the mixture. Season the chicken's exterior with
additional salt and freshly ground black pepper.
Place the chicken in a roasting pan or on a sheet
pan and roast for 15 minutes. Reduce the heat
to 375°F. Continue to cook the chicken until the
juice runs clear when tipping the carcass, about
1 hour. Cool the chicken at room temperature.
Once cooled, remove the skin and pick the
chicken with your fingers or with a fork, pulling the
meat into long strands. Discard the bones and skin.
Set the picked chicken aside. (This can be done a
day or two before preparing the salad.)

To prepare the dressing, combine the dry
mustard, ginger, garlic, soy sauce, and rice wine
vinegar in the bowl of a food processor. Blend
until very smooth. With the motor still running,

slowly drizzle in the sesame oil, the red wine
vinegar, and the peanut oil. (If the dressing looks
thick at this point, add a little cold water to thin it.)
Then gradually stream in the lime juice and honey.
Taste and season with salt and pepper. Pour the
dressing into a bowl and set aside.

To fry the wontons, heat the peanut oil in a large
pot to 375°F. Stack the wontons, and, with a
chef's knife, cut them into thin julienne strips.
Place the strips in the hot oil all at once and fry
until golden brown, about 2 minutes. With a
strainer, carefully remove the wonton strips from
the fryer and drain on paper towels. Drizzle with
salt while the wontons are still hot.

To assemble the salad, combine the cabbage,
carrots, daikon, red onion, red peppers, poblano
peppers, picked chicken, dressing, and about one-
third of the fried wontons in a large bowl. Season to
taste with salt and pepper. Mound the salad in the
center of individual plates. Top each mound with
the remaining fried wontons. Serve immediately.

Basil

460 King Street, downtown
(843) 724-3490
www.basilthairestaurant.com
Owners: Henry and Chai Eang
Chef: Suntorn Cherdchoongarm

A lime-green neon light topped with a 1950s-style bicycle serves as the distinctive beacon to the virgin restaurant venture of the brothers Eang (also of Chai's Lounge fame, see page 32), named simply and aptly Basil.

Thai restaurant extraordinaire, Basil throbs with the intensely fresh and pungent flavors of the Asian country. Lime, garlic, peppery heat, lemongrass, and more dapple the menu of noodles, satay, curries, and lovingly prepared combinations of assorted made-to-order sautés and salads, like Basil's signature Beef Larb (it is also prepared with chicken).

Basil hardly needs an introduction these days. Easily recognized as the best spot for authentic Thai in Charleston, equal parts of that reputation go to the brothers and Thailand native Suntorn Cherdchoongarm, universally referred to as "Chef" by the young and vibrant staff. He orchestrates the open kitchen like a maestro does a symphony. Woks flash, fire flickers, and noodles boil in a symphony of scents and sights that all but crackles with energy and the promise of tongue-tingling goodness that Basil somehow always delivers.

It's no small feat to wrangle a recipe from the fiercely proud chef, but Henry Eang was able to convince Suntorn to share his recipe for the restaurant's ultra-refreshing larb. Warm sautéed ground beef, doused with a dazzling arsenal of flavors—"citrus" or lime leaves, mint, scallions, cilantro, red onion, and, the mystery ingredient, seasoned ground rice—it's all wrapped up in leaves of fresh cabbage for a crunchy and unforgettable finish. Galangal, sweet rice, kaffir lime leaves, and lemongrass are specialty Thai ingredients available at Thai stores or online.

Beef Larb
(Serves 4)

For the rice powder:

1 teaspoon powdered galangal
½ cup uncooked sweet rice
½ cup uncooked jasmine rice
2 tablespoons kaffir lime leaves
2 tablespoons chopped fresh lemongrass

For the larb:

1 cup ground beef
2 teaspoons fresh-squeezed lemon juice
1½ teaspoons fish sauce
2 scallions, chopped
1 tablespoon chopped fresh cilantro
2 tablespoons chopped red onion
1 tablespoon chopped fresh mint
Salt and freshly ground black pepper to taste
½ head green cabbage, cut into 4 wedges
Lime wedges for garnish (optional)

To prepare the rice powder, combine all the ingredients and cook over low heat in a medium sauté pan, tossing occasionally, for 2 hours. When cool, grind in a food processor until the mixture becomes a fine powder. You'll need 1 teaspoon for the larb. (The remainder can be stored, like flour, at room temperature in an airtight container for several weeks.)

To prepare the larb, brown the beef in a large sauté pan over medium-high heat until thoroughly cooked, about 5 minutes. Remove from the heat and toss with the remaining ingredients (including 1 teaspoon of the rice powder) except for the cabbage.

To serve, distribute four servings of the warm beef larb on attractive plates. Garnish each with a wedge of fresh cabbage and a wedge of lime, if desired.

CHARLESTON SINGLE HOUSE

An architectural style designed to maximize cross-ventilating harbor breezes and privacy and to minimize Charleston's sometimes cruel heat and humidity, the Charleston Single House, in both its classic and modified versions, can be spotted all around the peninsula and, increasingly, in new subdivisions beyond.

A true Charleston Single House runs perpendicular to the front property line, and the side (the gabled smaller end) actually faces the street. The house is only one room deep, with two rooms on each floor. Though a door is normally positioned facing the street, the formal entrance to the house is situated midway along the piazza, which typically shades all stories (usually two or three) of the house. Often the piazza overlooks a private garden. To honor Charlestonians' storied sense of propriety, the neighboring house on the garden side has just a few windows facing the garden, to encourage peak piazza privacy.

THE GLASS ONION

1219 SAVANNAH HIGHWAY, WEST ASHLEY
(843) 225-1717
WWW.ILOVETHEGLASSONION.COM
PARTNERS/OWNERS: CHARLES VINCENT, CHRIS STEWART,
AND SARAH O'KELLEY

Though they hail from three different Southern states—Georgia, Alabama, and Louisiana—this trio of thirty-somethings stands united on what constitutes good cooking, something that is delivered in spades at The Glass Onion. Whether it's a grilled pimiento cheese po'boy on New Orleans bakery bread or Root Beer–Glazed Pork Belly with Grits and Greens, the theme here is high-quality nostalgic food at reasonable prices.

Though the food is Southern in style, its clarity is backed with experience in classical culinary technique and reverence for locally grown produce and hormone-free ingredients. Located on a busy highway in West Ashley, the restaurant has a breezy, sunny casualness punctuated with brown-paper-lined tables and a blackboard listing the day's seasonal specials. Orders are taken at the counter and little stands with pictures of notables from Elvis to Miss Piggy are settled on tables to help the kitchen deliver meals when they come up.

Glass Onion fans line up for the restaurant's chicken salad, which is either served on a plate with greens (as in this recipe) or thickly spread between two slices of Leidenheimer (of New Orleans) po'boy bread slathered with a layer of Duke's Mayonnaise. Charles has been guilty of playing with the recipe, born of a surplus of roasted chicken, by adding pickles and tarragon, but customers prefer to keep it simple, as it is here. The true goodness stems from the all-natural chicken from Springer Mountain Farms in north Georgia and the patience of the brining and roasting process. As for the mayo, Sarah says, like only a good Southern girl can, "It has to be Duke's." At the restaurant, chicken salad plates and sandwiches are garnished with house-made bread-and-butter pickles and a deviled egg. It simply doesn't get any more homey or satisfyingly Southern!

GLASS ONION ROASTED CHICKEN SALAD
(Serves 4 to 6)

For the brine:

5 cups kosher salt
2 cups granulated sugar
1 cup red pepper flakes
3 tablespoons whole black peppercorns
2 tablespoons fennel seeds
3 bay leaves
1 bunch fresh thyme
1 bunch fresh rosemary
1 head of garlic, top trimmed off
2 whole chickens (1–2 pounds)

For the salad:

Salt and freshly ground black pepper to coat
1 cup finely diced celery
1 cup Duke's Mayonnaise
1 cup Zatarain's Creole Mustard
1 tablespoon Crystal Hot Sauce
2 teaspoons red wine vinegar
Salt and freshly ground black pepper to taste
4–6 leaves crisp lettuce for garnish
12 tomato slices for garnish

In a large pot or stockpot, combine all of the brine ingredients except the chicken and bring to a simmer over high heat. Simmer until the salt and sugar dissolve, about 5 minutes. Remove from the heat and cool to room temperature. Submerge the chickens in the brine. Refrigerate, covered, for at least 4 hours and up to 24 hours, turning occasionally.

To make the chicken salad, preheat the oven to 400°F. Rub both brined chickens generously with salt and freshly ground black pepper. Place back side down on a large roasting pan and cook on the middle rack of the oven for about 1 hour, or until a thermometer reads 165°F in the inner part of the chicken thighs. Allow to cool to room temperature. Pull the meat from the bones, discarding the bones, fat, and skin. Break the chicken into bite-size pieces or strands, either by pulling with a fork or by chopping coarsely. In a large bowl, combine the remaining ingredients (except the garnishes) with the chicken and stir well with a wooden spoon to combine. Taste and adjust salt and pepper as needed. Serve a generous scoop of the chicken salad on each plate, garnished with a large leaf of fresh lettuce and several tomato slices.

PEARLZ OYSTER BAR

153 East Bay Street, downtown
(843) 577-5755
Executive Chef: Justin Strang

PEARLZ LITTLE OYSTER BAR

9 Magnolia Drive, West Ashley
(843) 573-2277
Executive Chef: Jamy Usher
WWW.PEARLZOYSTERBAR.COM

Raw bar indulgences and menu sophistication meet good times at these stellar restaurant siblings. Owned by TBONZ Restaurant Group, downtown's "big brother" Pearlz and West Ashley's "little brother" Pearlz share cool gustatory luster and a steady flow of beer and liquor—oyster and otherwise. Oyster-inspired art, including huge oyster murals sporting larger-than-life pearls, and distressed wood feel appropriately beachy. Pearlz's boisterous happy hours and savvy dinner menus make the restaurant twins a heavily favored destination for locals and tourists alike.

Easy-to-take prices on specialty oysters from Royal Miyagi to local selects and a diverse seafood-intensive menu complemented by a daily band of creative specials are instrumental components of Pearlz's formula. Justin Strang, executive chef at the downtown Pearlz, is a virtually self-taught chef who is motivated by fusion and American cooking and, in an unusual twist for an executive chef, baking. He personally makes all of the desserts, from White Chocolate Crème Brûlée to Peanut Butter Banana Pudding, and is a big fan of pairing chocolate with savory dishes, such as his signature White Chocolate Bourbon Barbecue Sauce with pork or beef fillet stuffed with dark chocolate. "I love inventing something that makes people smile. I just love that. I love it," he explains with infectious enthusiasm.

You'll love this blindingly beautiful and delicious structured salad, bursting with crab, topped with pepped-up mayonnaise, and drizzled with a sweet balsamic reduction.

CRABMEAT LOUIS

(Serves 4)

For the balsamic reduction sauce:

1 cup balsamic vinegar
¼ cup granulated sugar
Generous dash of fresh-squeezed lemon juice
3 tablespoons white wine vinegar
¼ cup cider vinegar

For the Louis dressing:

1 cup mayonnaise
¼ cup sweet chili sauce
1 teaspoon finely chopped chives
2 teaspoons fresh-squeezed lemon juice
1 tablespoon finely chopped fresh parsley
2 tablespoons minced scallions
Dash of Worcestershire sauce
1 teaspoon prepared horseradish
Salt and freshly ground black pepper to taste

For the salad:

1 cup julienned iceberg lettuce
1 cup diced tomatoes
½ cup finely diced hard-boiled egg
1 cup cubed avocado, tossed with 1/2 teaspoon
    fresh-squeezed lemon juice
½ cup claw crabmeat
½ cup lump crabmeat
16 spears fresh asparagus, briefly cooked in
    boiling salted water and instantly cooled
Fresh chives for garnish (optional)

Special equipment: four round stainless steel
    molds, 3½ inches wide and 2½ inches tall

To prepare the balsamic reduction, place all reduction ingredients in a medium saucepan and bring up to a simmer over medium-high heat. Once the liquid has reduced by half, remove from the heat and cool to room temperature. (The reduction can be stored in an airtight container in the refrigerator for several weeks.) Set aside.

To prepare the Louis dressing, combine all the ingredients in a medium bowl and whisk well to combine. Taste and adjust salt and pepper as needed. (The dressing can be made the night before and stored in an airtight container in the refrigerator until ready to use.)

To make the salad, the best plan is to have all of the ingredients prepped and lined up in an orderly mise en place and then assemble each of the four salads individually before plating. To begin, toss the iceberg lettuce with 2 tablespoons of the Louis dressing. Line each of the molds up on a small sheet pan. For each of the four salads, begin by firmly pressing ¼ cup of the tossed lettuce mixture into the bottom of each mold. Next, add a ¼ cup layer of diced tomatoes to each mold, pressing firmly. Follow with ⅛ cup of the hard-boiled egg, pressing firmly. Add ¼ cup of the lemon-tossed avocado to each mold, again pressing. Next, add to each 2 tablespoons of the claw crabmeat and follow with 2 tablespoons of the lump crabmeat, pressing firmly. Cover the molds tightly and refrigerate for at least 2 hours for the salad to set.

To plate the salads, gently push the layered salad through the molds onto the center of four individual plates. Be careful not to allow the salad to crumble! Cut the asparagus in half horizontally. For each plate, fan four of the spear tips in one corner and the spear bottoms in the opposite corner. Top the salads with 2 tablespoons of Louis dressing and, with a spoon, drizzle the balsamic reduction lightly back and forth across the plates.

ATLANTICVILLE RESTAURANT AND WINES

2063 MIDDLE STREET, SULLIVAN'S ISLAND
(843) 883-9452
WWW.ATLANTICVILLE.NET
EXECUTIVE CHEF: WILLIAM (BILLY) CONDON

Ambling like the dunes, grasses, and Atlantic Ocean that back up to this sleepy, beachy bungalow, Atlanticville wanders from one tiny dining room to the next while delivering a casually refined dining experience reflective of the distinctive heart and soul of Sullivan's Island.

Executive chef Billy Condon is a member of one of Charleston's restaurant dynasty families, but he maintains a strong sense of humility and a good sense of humor. "Don't call me Chef, just call me Billy," he regularly tells his staff and clients. A Charleston native, Billy found himself in the family business when two of his restaurateur cousins were looking for part-time summer help. Twenty years later and he's still at it, except instead of working for $7 an hour doing volume cooking, he's at Atlanticville's fine dining helm. Billy honed his cooking skills under the tutelage of former Atlanticville executive chef Phil Corr. "He was an absolute mentor to me," he recalls.

Billy carries on Phil's Thai Tuesday tradition. On warm evenings, this weekly food fest mostly takes place on the restaurant's spacious screened front porch, lit with colander lamps and hosting live music. Other days of the work week, Condon keeps busy "reinventing Southern dishes" and indulging his passion for working with fish. Atlanticville's warm goat cheese salad, an exceptionally edible study in crunchy and smooth contrasts, has been on the menu for years. "We've kept it because it's something people really like," says Billy.

Fried Goat Cheese Studded with Pistachios over Fancy Greens

(Serves 8)

For balsamic vinaigrette:

¼ cup balsamic vinegar
1 shallot, minced
1 teaspoon honey or granulated sugar
1 teaspoon Dijon mustard
Salt and freshly ground black pepper to taste
¾ cup virgin olive oil

For the goat cheese balls:

1 pound (about 3½ cups) goat cheese
   (Billy prefers Laurel Chenel brand),
   at room temperature
8 ounces cream cheese, at room temperature
½ teaspoon salt
1½ teaspoons freshly ground black pepper
1 tablespoon finely chopped fresh curly-leaf
   parsley
1 tablespoon finely chopped fresh thyme leaves
1 tablespoon finely chopped fresh tarragon
¼ cup pistachios, shelled and toasted
2 cups panko bread crumbs
1 teaspoon salt
2 eggs, beaten
2 cups whole milk
2 cups all-purpose flour
3 cups peanut oil

For the "fancy greens":

8–10 cups mesclun spring mix
Salt and freshly ground black pepper

To prepare the vinaigrette, blend together and emulsify the vinegar, shallot, sugar, mustard, and salt and pepper using a handheld immersion blender in a medium bowl. The vinaigrette can also be made using a food processor to emulsify and combine the olive oil in a steady stream. Season with salt and pepper and adjust seasonings as needed.

Next, prepare the goat cheese balls. In a large mixing bowl, combine both cheeses, salt, and ½ teaspoon pepper, blending well by hand. Add the fresh herbs and incorporate evenly throughout the cheese. Hand-roll the goat cheese mixture into 8 golf ball–sized balls. Chill in the refrigerator for at least 1 hour.

To prepare the bread crumb coating, combine the pistachios, panko bread crumbs, and 1 teaspoon each salt and freshly ground black pepper in the bowl of a food processor. Pulse several times, until the pistachios are broken into small nuggets. Meanwhile, in a small bowl, combine the eggs and milk and whisk well to combine. Place the flour and the bread crumb mixture in two separate shallow bowls. Line up the three bowls in this order: flour, egg wash, and pistachio mixture. Dip each cheese ball in the flour, followed by the egg wash, coating well, and finally roll the balls in the bread crumb mixture.

In a medium saucepan, heat the peanut oil to 360°F. In batches, fry the cheese balls until golden brown, 2 or 3 minutes. Reserve on paper towels.

To compose the salad, toss the greens with the vinaigrette in a large bowl. Season to taste with salt and pepper. Evenly distribute the greens in high mounds on each plate and top with a warm goat cheese ball. Serve immediately.

Soups

In Charleston, women don't (heaven forbid) "sweat," nor do they "perspire." They "glow." But even though there is plenty of glowing going on come August, when temperatures hover around 100°F and the humidity flirts with 100 percent, Charlestonians love their soup. Hot or cold, winter or summer, it's a menu requisite. In her foreword to *Two Hundred Years of Charleston Cooking,* Elizabeth Verner Hamilton refers to "the Charleston habit of serving a properly balanced dinner of soup, rice and gravy, meat, two vegetables and a dessert at two or preferably 3 o'clock."

This tradition dates back to colonial times, but the city's modern chefs continue to put new twists on old favorites like she-crab soup. The ubiquitous Lowcountry classic was first created in Charleston, and Virginia's on King's heavenly version takes cues from a long-guarded family recipe. Farther downtown, young chef Aaron Deal casts a cool and verdant spin with his elegantly structured Cucumber Gazpacho and Alluette's Café serves up a sweet and soulful Lima Bean Soup, daring to go where no Southerner has dared to go before: Alluette's soup is pork-free.

ALLUETTE'S CAFÉ

80 REID STREET, DOWNTOWN (UPPER NECK)
(843) 577-6926
WWW.ALLUETTES.COM
CHEF-OWNER: ALLUETTE JONES

Ask this former automobile salesperson, cancer survivor, and self-described "Geechi Girl" a direct question and you will get a direct answer: "I call myself Geechi girl because I *am* a Geechi girl! I'm from the Lowcountry in South Carolina. My accent is Gullah" (see sidebar, page 67). "I'm just Geechi," she giggles, her pink paisley-patterned glasses bouncing merrily along the bridge of her nose.

Alluette prides herself on her Lowcountry origins and African-American heritage, but a hearty work ethic, pork-free cooking (practically unheard of in the South), and good karma are also primary ingredients at this "holistic soul food" kitchen, otherwise known as Alluette's Café. The apricot-tinted cinder-block walls of the homey and intimate dining room open to a spacious outdoor patio adorned with friendly-looking sunflowers and eclectic chairs, just begging for al fresco dining on any one of Charleston's many sunny days. Alluette greets everyone who enters the place with a huge smile and a warm hello and urges them to make themselves at home. Meanwhile, she practically single-handedly (husband, Cliff, is usually at her side) prepares "Hey Y'All" Savory Sardines with Caramelized Onions, her signature shrimp salad and egg salad sandwiches, and savor-steeped soups and salads.

Alluette's lima bean soup, made from organic dried beans, contains only five ingredients but is packed with simple Southern flavor and the kick of cayenne. It's surprisingly sweet and clean tasting, which Alluette attributes to the absence of pork. She recommends using filtered water, but it's not essential for success. "Patience and goodness are," advises Alluette.

LIMA BEAN SOUP
(Serves 6 to 8)

2 cups dried organic lima beans
3 cloves garlic
8 cups filtered water or "way more than
   enough to cover"
6 sprigs fresh thyme
Sea salt and cayenne pepper, to taste

Bring all the ingredients to a boil in a large pot and simmer vigorously for about 1 hour, keeping in mind that beans that have been stored longer than 1 year may take a little longer to soften. Reduce heat to low and simmer for another 20 to 30 minutes or until the beans are soft but still firm enough to hold their shape. Remove the thyme sprigs. Taste and adjust salt and cayenne pepper as needed. Serve hot with a few sprigs of thyme as garnish.

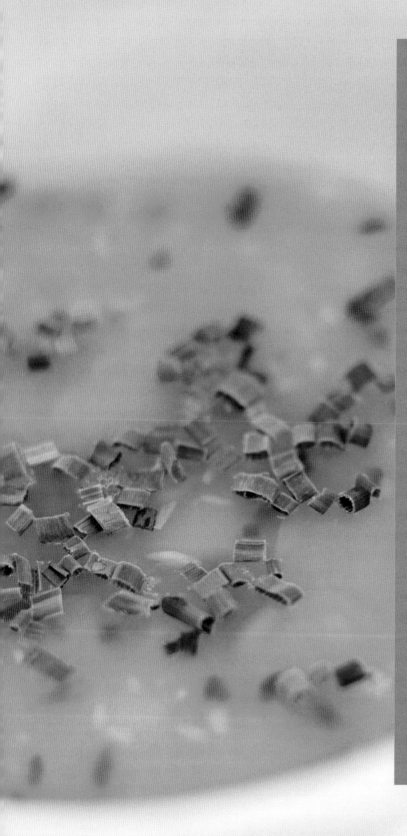

STEADY YUH HEAD

That's Gullah-speak for "think hard for the answer." The question, then, has to be, what exactly are Gullah and Geechee (also spelled "Geechi")? According to Charleston-based Gullah guru Alphonso Brown, both are names for a language and culture born in Africa. "*Gullah* derives from 'Gola' and *Geechee* comes from 'Kissi' (pronounced geezee). Both were tribes living in and around Sierra Leone in West Africa," explains the licensed Gullah tour guide and author of *A Guide to Gullah Charleston.* "More than 40 percent of Africans entering America came through Charleston harbor," says Brown. Many of the slaves who remained in the Lowcountry were from the rice-rich production areas of West Africa. Their skills were used to fuel the wealth of rice plantation owners here. The slaves' tolerance to malaria (which drove many wealthy whites away during peak season) and ability to congregate in slave-exclusive communities (especially in remote pockets of the barrier islands) allowed the slaves and their descendants to continue many of their cultural traditions and preserve their own language.

According to Brown, Gullah was a result of African Americans trying to learn English without being formally taught. "We were trying to speak good English. People always ask me how I learned to speak Gullah. I say, no, how did I get to learn English? English is my second language," Brown says. Cultural traditions, such as the art of weaving sweetgrass baskets, and gumbo (a derivative of an African word for "okra"), an okra stew, continue in the Lowcountry to this day.

Grace Episcopal Tea Room

98 Wentworth Street, downtown
(843) 723-4575
WWW.GRACECHURCHCHARLESTON.ORG

Wisteria and Confederate jasmine aside, nothing puts spring in Charleston's step more than the annual eleven-day-long rite of passage that is the Grace Episcopal Tea Room. Run in tandem with Spoleto Festival USA (the city's annual cultural and art festival), this "restaurant" is housed within the walls of a graceful historic church (established circa 1848) and the "chefs" are the ladies and gentlemen of the parish. Though ephemeral, it's an experience not to be missed. There are a few other tea rooms around town this time of year, but this one's the titan of sweet tea and all things Charlestonian. "Our menu is okra soup, shrimp remoulade, crab soup, etc. They all have the flavor of the Lowcountry, but they're original," explains Mary Bradley, the tea room chairperson. Many of the recipes come from the family recipe boxes of the church members who prepare them. Locals and visitors alike flock to share in their goodness while it lasts (from Memorial Day through ten weekdays and the middle Saturday of Spoleto).

Expect to see a handsome gentleman host clad in full-on Charleston regalia: a seersucker suit, a dandy bow tie, a fresh magnolia boutonniere, and a broad-rimmed straw boater. He'll escort ladies to their tables as a piano man plays gentle tunes in the background. And just when you think it can't get any more deliciously Southern, you're reminded that all proceeds (over $300,000 total since the tea room's 1992 debut) are designated for select area outreach programs.

This rich, meaty crab soup is a huge crowd pleaser. "We do three pots every morning; that's enough to serve 150 people," says Mary. After tweaking an old recipe from Everett's Restaurant (now defunct), the church ladies finally found the magic touch: Old Bay Seasoning. Serve the soup steaming hot and don't forget to pass a cruet of sherry along with it. That would be blasphemy.

CRAB SOUP
(Serves 10)

1 pound fresh (or frozen) blue crab claw meat
5 tablespoons butter
1 cup finely chopped onion
1 cup finely chopped celery
1 quart whole milk
1 quart heavy cream
1 quart half-and-half
¼–½ cup cornstarch
Generous dash of Worcestershire sauce
3 tablespoons sherry or to taste
1 tablespoon Old Bay Seasoning or to taste
Salt and freshly ground black pepper to taste

Pick over the crabmeat. Remove and discard all cartilage or shell bits. In a large pot, melt the butter over medium heat. Add the onion and celery, stirring to coat, and cook until softened and translucent, about 3 minutes. Add 3 cups of the milk, the cream, and the half-and-half. Heat to just boiling, stirring often. Dissolve ¼ cup cornstarch plus 1 to 2 tablespoons for a thicker soup in the remaining 1 cup of milk and add to the soup, stirring well. Add the Worcestershire sauce, sherry, Old Bay Seasoning, and salt and pepper. Taste and adjust salt and pepper accordingly. When the soup is thickened (thickened enough to coat a spoon, about 20 minutes), add the crabmeat. Heat through over low heat. Thin with more heavy cream or half-and-half before serving if the soup is too thick as well as to "stretch for extra servings." Serve hot.

CHARLESTON'S VERY OWN TEA PARTY

Unlike their revolutionary compatriots in Boston, Charlestonians thought better of dumping tea into the Charleston harbor. Instead, they stored their overly taxed (without representation) tea in the cellar of the downtown Old Exchange Building where, a few years later, in 1776, South Carolina would sign her first Constitution and declare independence from Great Britain.

"The tea was later sold and used to fund the coffers of the newborn state. I think it's a wonderful story," says Denise LeCroy, a self-professed tea enthusiast and tea historian. A century later, Charleston would become home to what remains the only commercial tea plantation in North America, the Charleston Tea Plantation, currently situated on Wadmalaw Island, about thirty minutes from downtown. The tea plantation produces a black tea called American Classic that has officially been declared the hospitality beverage of the state of South Carolina. As if all that weren't enough to topple the crumpet cart, a twentieth-century visit to Charleston by author Owen Wister and a love-inspiring nibble of Lady Baltimore Cake here led him to write the story of Lady Baltimore, based on the woman who served him his first slice, says LeCroy.

Virginia's on King

412 King Street, downtown
(843) 735-5800
www.virginiasonking.com
Executive Chef: Jason Murphy

Whether sitting down for a noon meal ("lunch" elsewhere but "dinner" at Virginia's) or for an evening meal ("dinner" elsewhere but "supper" at Virginia's), guests here can expect a heaping serving of authentic Charleston-born gentility and truly Southern gustatory pleasures. Country Fried Steak Served with Red-Eye Gravy, Stuffed Pork Chops, Fried Pickles, and Brown Sugar–Glazed Ham and more come directly from the recipe file of the restaurant's namesake, one Mrs. Virginia Bennett. A native of Charleston, Mrs. Bennett believes in the tradition of breaking bread and sharing good food with her large brood. For years, she, her six children, and husband Warren J. convened in their home to dine on Sunday afternoons (which later become Thursday afternoons) for a multigenerational family dinner.

Now, everyone's invited to share in the tasty tradition, which is served seven days a week at the restaurant. Executive chef Jason Murphy literally sat down with Virginia to look over every single one of her recipes and tweak as needed. As luscious as the food is (especially the fried okra with house-made remoulade that will leave you crying for more), the smart, mercifully gingham-free décor is not to be overlooked. Guess who had a say in all of that that? If you look around on a Thursday afternoon, you might just see the grand dame herself.

Virginia's She-Crab Soup
(Serves 10 to 12)

2 sticks (½ pound) sweet butter
2 small carrots, peeled and cut into fine even dice
1 onion, cut into fine even dice
1 large stalk celery, cut into fine even dice
½ cup plus 3 tablespoons sherry
½ cup all-purpose flour
3 quarts heavy cream
2 tablespoons Worcestershire sauce
2 tablespoons hot sauce (preferably Frank's Hot Sauce)
3 tablespoons chopped fresh parsley
3 tablespoons chopped fresh thyme
1 bay leaf
½ pound crab roe
½ pound fresh blue crab meat
1 tablespoon honey
Salt and white pepper to taste

In a large soup pot, melt the butter over medium heat. Add the carrots, onion, and celery. Stir to coat and cook until the vegetables have softened, about 5 minutes. Increase heat to medium-high and add ½ cup of sherry (reserving the rest for later). Stir and cook until the sherry has reduced by half. Stir in the flour to create a roux. Cook the roux over medium-low heat (do not allow it to color), until it has thickened and formed a loose paste, 3 to 5 minutes. Add the heavy cream, whisking to incorporate with the roux. Cook over medium heat until the soup base has thickened, about 10 minutes. Add the remaining ingredients and cook another 20 minutes, or until the soup has thickened enough to slightly coat the back of a spoon and the crab is cooked. Taste and adjust salt and pepper as needed. Discard the bay leaf. Serve in shallow bowls that showcase the soup's silky texture and pale pink blush. If desired, garnish each soup with a drizzle of the remaining sherry.

THE ORIGINS OF SHE-CRAB SOUP

The creation of she-crab soup is widely attributed to the butler and cook of early-twentieth-century Charleston mayor R. Goodwyn Rhett. Later to become a celebrated cook and restaurant chef, the former butler/cook named William Deas was assigned a daunting task by the mayor's wife: to gussy up plain old crab. His trick was to add the orange- or pink-hued crab eggs that give the bisque or chowder its pretty, feminine pinkness and distinctive flavor (which is altogether different from Grace Episcopal Tea Room's peanut-butter hued and nutty version, page 69). Jason Murphy recommends using blue crab meat and blue crab roe and drizzling in sherry just before serving.

THE RESTAURANT AT MIDDLETON PLACE

MIDDLETON PLACE
4300 ASHLEY RIVER ROAD, WEST ASHLEY
(843) 556-6020
WWW.MIDDLETONPLACE.ORG
EXECUTIVE CHEF: MICAH GARRISON

Set on the hauntingly beautiful historic grounds of Middleton Plantation, the restaurant offers a feast for the senses as much as it does for the soul. The physical vestiges of what was one of Charleston's greatest rice plantations during the seventeenth and eighteenth centuries dot the sixty-acre landscape, lush with low-hanging live oaks and impeccable lawns and gardens. The visual stars here are a cascading staircase of verdant terraces leading down to the Ashley River and the rice beds that helped make the Middleton clan so sinfully wealthy. The Civil War (referred to more commonly in these parts as "the War of Northern Aggression") would put an end to all that and cause the destruction of the main house. The ruins and some outbuildings remain, but the showstoppers are the grounds and, of course, the restaurant.

The restaurant is housed in a small brick outbuilding that overlooks a graveyard where some of the Middleton slaves are buried and offers a sumptuous view of Rice Mill Pond. By day, an opportunity to dine is included with the price of admission to the museum. The restaurant's menu was originally created by recipe consultant and Middleton's longtime chef in residence, Edna Lewis. Executive chef Micah Garrison remains true to Edna's quintessentially Charleston recipes, including Huguenot Torte and shrimp and grits, particularly for the lunch menu. He dresses up dinner for the night crowd, issuing forth his insightful interpretations of Southern cooking.

In addition to the historic working environment, Micah draws inspiration from the organic garden on the grounds. For his okra and tomato gumbo, he advises using the freshest vegetables possible. "Don't try and reinvent the wheel. Technique and freshness work wonders," he says. This thick, fragrant soup is typically served over rice—a truly Charleston staple if ever there was one!

Okra Gumbo
(Serves 10)

2 tablespoons vegetable oil

5 stalks celery, cut into ¼-inch dice

2 large carrots, peeled and cut into ¼-inch dice

1 large onion, cut into ¼-inch dice

3 cups fresh corn, cut from the cob
   (or substitute frozen)

2½ cups fresh butter beans (or substitute
   frozen; see sidebar below)

Salt to taste

2 cups tomato paste

2 teaspoons ground cumin

2 quarts high-quality vegetable stock

3 cups canned diced tomatoes with juice

8 cups fresh okra, cut into ½-inch-thick slices

2 tablespoons gumbo filé (see sidebar below)

Freshly ground black pepper to taste

Heat a large soup pot over medium-high heat. Add the oil, celery, carrots, onion, corn, and butter beans with a pinch of salt. Cook, stirring, until the onion becomes translucent, about 5 minutes. Stir in the tomato paste and cumin, cooking briefly. Add the vegetable stock and diced tomatoes. Bring soup to a simmer. When the carrots are softened but still al dente, add the okra and gumbo filé. Simmer for about 15 minutes, or until the okra is softened and the gumbo has thickened. Season to taste with salt and pepper. Serve immediately, or better yet, serve the next day. Micah says it's better that way.

MYSTERY INGREDIENTS—BUTTER BEANS AND GUMBO FILÉ

Unless you're from the South, butter beans and gumbo filé may be entirely new to you. Embrace both! *Butter Bean* is the perfect name for the pale green (or sometimes speckled) legume that thrives during Charleston's long, hot summer months. Its smooth, even flavor and soft, yielding flesh recalls creamery-fresh butter. The beans are used in everything from soups to salads. If you have trouble finding them, the slightly larger lima bean will make a fine substitute. Gumbo filé hails from Cajun country and is made of ground sassafras leaves. It is used here to both season and thicken the soup. Look for it in Cajun specialty stores or online.

39 Rue de Jean

39 John Street, downtown
(843) 722-8881
www.39ruedejean.com
Executive Chef: Jason Murphy

Beautifully honed to resemble an antique Parisian brasserie, 39 Rue de Jean (known to locals as "Rue") has universal appeal. Beefy house-ground burgers and steak frites comingle with delicate moules and hearty coq au vin to satisfy a kind of everyman hunger, yet Rue stays close to her Parisian roots. The young, attractive staff wear black and the waitresses look prêt-à-porter in their ruffled white aprons. Located in a former warehouse (built circa 1880), Rue has an authentic brasserie patina and glows with distressed mirrors, chocolate mahogany booths, old brick walls, and a bar imported from France.

There, if you're lucky, you'll spot a bartender named Smoak with an uncanny ability to remember anyone's favorite drink—from the time you place your first order until you place your last. A true neighborhood corner in the happening Upper King Street area (the stretch of King between Calhoun and Spring Streets) of downtown, Rue has changed ownership and a chef or two since its opening nearly a decade ago, but it has never wavered from its mostly Francophile mission. The Onion Soup Gratinée, Rue's second biggest seller, is a prime example. At the restaurant, it's prepared with equal parts house-made veal stock and chicken stock, swimming in a sea of sweet, caramelized onions kissed with sherry and topped with imported Gruyère brought to bubbling goodness in a hot oven.

Because it's easier to find high-quality prepared beef stock and beef bones to make your own stock, this recipe calls for beef stock instead of veal stock. Whatever you do, don't skimp on the principal components—a good stock (preferably homemade and salt-free), well-caramelized onions, and Gruyère cheese—and your Onion Soup Gratinée will taste just as authentically delicious as the version Jason Murphy brews for the Rue crew.

Onion Soup Gratinée
(Serves 8 to 10)

2 tablespoons olive oil
10 large yellow onions, thinly sliced
2 cups sodium-free chicken stock
2 cups sodium-free beef stock
2 tablespoons brandy

2 tablespoons sherry
Salt to taste
25 slices baguette, diagonally cut and toasted
25 slices Gruyère cheese

Heat a large soup pot over medium-high heat. Add the olive oil and heat. When the pan is hot, add the onions. Stirring constantly to prevent burning, reduce the heat to medium. Keep cooking and caramelizing the onions until they begin to brown and "all the natural sugars are out," 10 to 15 minutes. Remove from the heat and allow to cool for 10 minutes. Add the chicken stock and beef stock and bring the mixture to a boil over high heat. Add the brandy and sherry. Season to taste with salt.

To serve, preheat the oven to 400°F. Ladle the hot soup into deep ovenproof soup bowls (or bistro bowls), leaving room for the toast and cheese. Top each with two or three toast points and two or three slices Gruyère cheese. Bake the soup in the bowls for 8 to 10 minutes or until the cheese is brown and bubbly. Serve immediately.

Circa 1886

149 Wentworth Street, downtown
(843) 853-7828
www.circa1886.com
Executive Chef: Marc Collins

The year 1886 was a rough one for Charleston. With the town still reeling from the devastating financial and structural ruin of the Civil War, an earthquake had the audacity to roll through, killing an estimated sixty people and sending many a building tumbling down. Not so for the stalwart mansion at 149 Wentworth Street (now a AAA Five Diamond hotel known as the Wentworth Mansion). The home of a wealthy sulfur magnate at a time when nearly everyone else in Charleston was poor, it was constructed the same year as the earthquake. It's rumored, according to Marc Collins, that the cupola of the imposing brick structure was built expressly so the owner could "look down" on all of Charleston, but it was more likely a spotting post for the fire department. Either way, the owner probably wasn't a terribly popular guy among the "too poor to paint, too proud to whitewash" set.

Circa 1886 is housed in the mansion's original carriage house. Marc keeps the restaurant's menu and mood universe small and uniquely Charleston. "When I sit down to write recipes, I write with Charleston's influences from 200 years ago, when it was such a large port city. The spice trade, slavery, French Huguenot, Caribbean flavors—they're all melded into the menu," he explains. Dishes like Spicy Grilled Shrimp over Fried Green Tomatoes with Chowchow and Carolina Crab Cake Soufflé with Mango Puree, Pineapple Relish, and Crispy Sweet Potatoes are always on the menu at the lusciously antique restaurant with sage green cypress paneling and intimate arched booths. At Circa 1886, this soup is frequently served as an amuse-bouche to jump-start lucky guests' dinners.

Peanut Soup
(Serves 6 to 8)

1 tablespoon olive oil or vegetable oil
1 cup diced celery
1 cup diced onion
1 cup raw or dry-roasted peanuts, plus finely
   chopped peanuts for garnish (optional)
3 tablespoons soy sauce
3 tablespoons rice wine vinegar
1 tablespoon Tabasco sauce
2 quarts chicken stock
1 cup peanut butter
Salt to taste
Chili oil for garnish (optional)

Heat the oil in a soup pot over medium heat. Add the celery and onion and stir. Cook gently until translucent, 3 to 5 minutes. Add the peanuts and cook for 4 minutes, stirring frequently. Add the soy sauce, vinegar, Tabasco sauce, and stock. Continue simmering until the peanuts are soft, about 30 minutes. Strain the soup to separate the liquids from the solids, reserving both separately. Puree the vegetable and peanut solids in a blender or food processor, adding just enough liquid to cover the puree. Slowly add the rest of the liquid while pureeing.

Return the soup to the stove and bring to a simmer. Whisk in the peanut butter, heat through, adjust salt as needed, and serve. Garnish with a sprinkle of finely chopped peanuts or a drop or two of chili oil, if desired.

Lana Restaurant & Bar

210 Rutledge Avenue, downtown
(843) 720-8899
www.lanarestaurant.com
Executive Chef/Co-Owner: John Ondo

Though he's spent nearly twenty years in the restaurant business, John Ondo could have just as easily been a professional comedian. When asked what title he goes by, his joking retort is "lead donkey," but in fact, he is much more than that. A native of Charleston, John works in tandem with the other co-owner, Bosnia native Drazen Romic, to issue their special brand of cooking—what Ondo calls "new Mediterranean." "All of our dishes are about getting the best local stuff and putting a Euro twist on it. The steak is French, the chicken is Spanish, and the lamb shank is Italian. They're each grounded in the flavors of a specific Mediterranean country," he explains. John and Drazen set up shop in the battered and half-ruined remains of a former fish market to create Lana, doing much of the demolition and new construction themselves. All the décor for the five-year-old restaurant, from the muted mushroom color scheme to the deep padded banquettes, had to be cleared by Drazen's nearly eighty-year-old mother.

On most days and nights, you'll find the staggeringly tall (six feet and six inches) Drazen working the front of the house while John peeps his handsome carrot-top through the small window of the small kitchen that serves the big, sun-kissed dishes of the Mediterranean, such as Lamb Spanakopita and Basque Chicken. Baccaula is a Spanish-style fish soup with a tomato and saffron base. It is simultaneously spicy, savory, and slightly sweet and it's a regular player on Lana's menu. Traditionally it's prepared with salt cod, but John says it works just as well with fresh cod "or any kind of moist, white fish such as grouper, flounder, or red snapper."

SOPA BACCAULA
(Serves 8 to 10)

½ cup extra-virgin olive oil
1 cup finely chopped onion
½ cup peeled and finely chopped carrots
½ cup finely chopped celery
4 cloves garlic, finely chopped
Pinch of saffron
1 teaspoon red pepper flakes, plus more to taste
Pinch of dried thyme leaves
Pinch of ground oregano
Pinch of Spanish paprika
1 cup dry white wine
Salt and freshly ground black pepper to taste
1 28-ounce can whole tomatoes or 10 medium
   tomatoes, peeled, seeded, and diced
3 cups fish stock or chicken stock
2 pounds cod or other moist white fish,
   coarsely chopped
¼ cup finely chopped flat-leaf parsley
Croutons for serving (optional)

In a large heavy-bottomed stockpot, heat the olive oil over medium heat. Add the onion, carrots, celery, and garlic and cook, stirring, until softened and translucent, about 5 minutes. Add the saffron, red pepper flakes, thyme, oregano, and paprika. Stir (this will help the saffron "bloom" and release its flavor) and cook for another 3 minutes. Add the white wine and lightly season with salt and pepper. Increase the heat to medium-high. Once the wine has reduced by half, add the tomatoes and stock. Bring to a boil, then reduce to a simmer and allow the soup to cook for 1 hour. Remove the soup from the stove and puree until smooth in a blender or food processor or with a standing handheld immersion blender. To finish, return the soup to the stove. Add the fish and parsley. Bring to a boil, then reduce to a simmer and cook through, about 20 minutes. Taste and adjust seasoning (including red pepper flakes) as needed. Serve hot. This soup is delicious with oven-toasted croutons for dipping.

TRISTAN

55 SOUTH MARKET STREET, DOWNTOWN
(843) 534-2155
WWW.TRISTANDINING.COM
EXECUTIVE CHEF: AARON DEAL

Like a cosmopolitan culinary fun house, Tristan rides on waves of primary colors and sophisticated glam. Situated in the heart of the tourist-rich Old City Market area (see sidebar, page 83) of downtown, Tristan (like nearby Peninsula Grill, Hank's, Mercato, and Anson) stands out as a beacon of excellence in a bland sea of choices crafted for the less-discerning masses. And, Tristan offers an exceptional three-course prix fixe lunch.

At the nucleus of Tristan's creative maelstrom is one of the town's youngest notable chefs. Not yet thirty, Aaron Deal ditched an initial foray into university-level computer science studies for summa cum laude honors and a degree from Johnson & Wales. Aaron refers to his style as "new American" and deals it out in sensibly and flavorfully layered dishes such as Heirloom Baby Beets with Split Creek Chèvre Mousseline and Sunflower Seeds Pistou. Echoing the lollipop colors of the restaurant, Aaron leans toward youth and whimsy in his presentations, but he keeps his eye on clarity. "I want my guests to look at their plates and expect to get the flavors even before eating. If they see a zucchini puree, they should expect to taste zucchini in a big way," says Aaron.

This recipe for Cucumber Gazpacho reveals Aaron's penchant for pickling ("It is a way of introducing new flavor dimensions to a dish that a splash of vinegar or lemon wouldn't offer," he says) and beautiful plating. At Tristan, the pickled shrimp, avocado, and fromage blanc are pre-assembled in deep oval soup "boats" and brought to the table, where they're topped off with the brilliantly green and cool gazpacho. "I recommend people do it the same way at home. It shows an extra step," says Aaron. All three components of this cool, refreshing soup can be prepared separately, at least one day ahead, and plated at the last minute. This fact, combined with the soup's good looks, make this recipe a star pick for entertaining.

CUCUMBER GAZPACHO WITH FROMAGE BLANC, PETITE CILANTRO, PICKLED WILD SHRIMP, AND AVOCADO
(Serves 6 to 8)

For the fromage blanc:

1 quart whole milk
½ cup heavy cream
1 cup buttermilk
1 tablespoon lemon juice

For the pickled shrimp:

1 cup rice wine vinegar
1 bay leaf
¼ cup granulated sugar
¼ cup honey
1 tablespoon salt
1 tablespoon whole coriander seeds
1½ cups water
1 pound fresh large shrimp (26–30 count),
    peeled and deveined

For the cucumber gazpacho:

2 pounds (about 8) English cucumbers, peeled
    and coarsely chopped
2 green bell peppers, seeded and quartered
1 yellow onion, coarsely chopped
2 cloves garlic
1 teaspoon honey
3 tablespoons coarsely chopped fresh cilantro
3 tablespoons coarsely chopped fresh basil
1 tablespoon coarsely chopped fresh mint
Kosher salt and freshly ground white pepper
    to taste

To garnish:

18–20 thin avocado slices (from 1 avocado)
12 to 14 leaves fresh cilantro

First prepare the fromage blanc. In a heavy-bottomed saucepan, combine the milk and heavy cream. Separately, combine the buttermilk and lemon juice in either a measuring cup or a small bowl. Pour the buttermilk and lemon juice mixture into the saucepan and heat over medium heat until the mixture reaches 175°F, stirring only twice. Once it has reached 175°F, remove the saucepan from the heat and allow to sit, undisturbed, for 10 minutes. Line a colander with cheesecloth and strain the contents of the saucepan over the sink. Squeeze and twist the ends of the cheesecloth, tying with kitchen string to secure. Hang the cheese overnight over a bowl by tying the string to a cabinet knob or from a high refrigerator shelf with a bowl underneath to catch the dripping liquid, and refrigerate. Additional liquid will drain from the cheese. This can be discarded.

To prepare the pickled shrimp, bring all pickling ingredients except the shrimp to a simmer in a medium saucepan over medium-high heat. Once simmering, cook for an additional 1 minute. Meanwhile, place the shrimp in a nonreactive container, such as a glass container or bowl. Pour the hot pickling liquid over the shrimp. It will cook the shrimp while infusing them with the flavors of the pickling liquid. Once the liquid is cooled, store the shrimp refrigerated in the liquid and covered for at least 8 and up to 24 hours before using. Drain and discard liquid after the pickling process.

To prepare the cucumber gazpacho, fill a medium saucepan three-quarters full with cold water. Bring to a boil over high heat. Meanwhile, puree the cucumber, green pepper, onion, garlic, and honey together in a blender until thoroughly pureed. When the water is boiling, add the fresh cilantro, basil, and mint and blanch for 30 seconds. Strain herbs and shock them in a bowl of ice water. (This helps stop the cooking and preserve color and flavor.) Reserve 1 cup of the blanching liquid. To finish the soup, add the strained herbs and the reserved blanching liquid to the blender and puree together with the vegetable mixture. Strain the gazpacho through a fine-mesh strainer or chinois. Season to taste with salt and white pepper. Store overnight or until ready to serve.

To plate the soup, slice each shrimp in half on the bias. They will still appear whole, but the cut will create easy bite-sized pieces. For each individual serving, top a slice of avocado with a dollop of fromage blanc and a sliced shrimp. Make three such piles in the bottom of each dish and top with a few cilantro leaves. To serve, bring each plate to the table and—before your guests' very eyes—top each with approximately ¾ cup of the gazpacho, poured from a large pitcher.

THE OLD CITY MARKET

Between Meeting and East Bay Streets in the heart of downtown is a string of our open-air brick buildings that bulge with incongruous bedfellows—kitschy curios, packaged foodstuffs, and beautiful sweetgrass baskets. Open seven days a week and surrounded by several carriage tour companies, restaurants, and shops, it's a frequent tourist haunt. For that reason, along with a dearth of easy parking, many locals avoid the area. Yet everyone should go—at least once. There are many (often negotiable) roses to be found among the useless thorns, and the hustle and bustle is inspiring when the mood is right. The main building of the market is called Market Hall. Built in 1841, it is now home to the Daughters of the Confederacy Museum. In the old days, the market area was a vending area for local seafood, meats, vegetables, and fruits. It has been hotly debated whether it should return to its original purpose and be closed off to cars in an effort to lure more regular local traffic. For now, you know where to get lunch.

Magnolias

185 East Bay Street, downtown
(843) 577-7771
www.magnolias-blossom-cypress.com
Founding Executive Chef: Donald Barickman
Executive Chef: Don Drake

Donald Barickman is widely recognized as the leader of Charleston's culinary renaissance, which most agree began with the opening of this restaurant shortly after the calamity that was Hurricane Hugo in 1989. Ironically, the storm put Charleston on the national awareness map and also led to a flood of insurance money that helped fuel the city's growth and prosperity. Donald, a young chef and recent Culinary Institute of America grad at the time, turned heads and dropped jaws with his groundbreaking notion of serving grits—widely considered breakfast fare—all day long in a white linen restaurant. And he had the audacity to cook them with stock, cream, and butter.

Two decades later, Donald's signature touch shines on the menu, which he describes as "creative work with Southern staples like rice, grits, corn, and beans." He's since been relegated to corporate work as vice president of the restaurant's parent company, Hospitality Management Group, Inc. (The group also owns Blossom, page 126, and Cypress, page 168). Despite his busy schedule, he still devotes time to the kitchen, regularly partnering with executive chef Don Drake to create daily specials. Loyal patrons populate the pretty, spacious restaurant decorated with swaths of the forged iron magnolias for which it's named.

This dish—"which melds all of the flavors of the South into a chowder like none other"—is vintage Barickman. He came up with it after finding some cured ham trimmings on a cold winter afternoon when his dad, for whom he named the dish, was in town. "I found those and grabbed some collards, potatoes, and tomatoes and went home and put it together," he explains. This recipe has also been featured in *Martha Stewart Living and The Best American Recipes 2003–2004* cookbook and by Turner South Network on *Blue Ribbon*.

Elwood's Ham Chowder
(Serves 12)

1 tablespoon vegetable oil, plus more if needed
1 pound cured ham trimmings, coarsely ground
  or minced
3 cups diced onions
2 tablespoons sliced garlic
12 cups stemmed and finely chopped
  fresh collards
1½ tablespoons chopped fresh thyme
2 tablespoons chopped fresh parsley

1 28-ounce can whole tomatoes with juice
7 cups chicken stock
2 cups beef stock, homemade or high-quality
  store-bought
6 cups diced red potatoes (¼-inch) dice
1½ teaspoons freshly ground black pepper
1½ teaspoons Tabasco sauce, plus more
  to taste
Salt to taste

Heat the oil in a large, heavy pot. Add the ham and render the fat from the ham, cooking it slowly over medium heat and stirring frequently to keep it from browning. Add the onions and garlic. Reduce heat to low and continue to cook, stirring occasionally, until the onions and garlic are soft, 3 minutes. Add more oil if the ham doesn't render enough fat to keep the pan moist. Slowly add the collards and allow them to wilt. (This should be done in two batches, as the collards are very bulky, but will wilt down like all greens.) Add the herbs, tomatoes with juice, chicken stock, beef stock, and red potatoes. Slowly bring mixture up to a simmer and continue to cook for 20 to 30 minutes, or until the potatoes are cooked through. Skim the chowder to remove any foam or oil that may appear during cooking. Add the pepper and Tabasco. Season to taste with salt and more Tabasco if desired.

Sandwiches

John Montagu, the Fourth Earl of Sandwich, for whom the sandwich is thought to have been named, would surely be surprised by the diversity and popularity his favorite bread-enveloped snack has achieved since the eighteenth century. So much more than something to wrap up cold meats or keep hands free while eating, sandwiches these days are round-the-clock hunger-stomping staples.

Coincidentally, Montagu is a big name in Charleston. It (and a variation on the theme) is the name of two major thoroughfares here, a testament to Charleston's Huguenot past and present. One might predict a preponderance of dainty crustless cocktail-party shrimp, egg salad, and chicken salad sandwiches on Charleston's restaurant menus, but the opposite is true. Gargantuan portions fit for the famished and gourmet touches fit for a king (let alone an earl) abound. Jack's Cosmic Dogs goes galactic with hot dogs topped with crunchy blue cheese slaw and slathered with sweet potato mustard. Poe's Tavern takes burgers to eerily delicious heights with its "Sleeper" burger of 100 percent certified Angus chuck decked out with buffalo shrimp and roasted garlic blue cheese. The classic BLT gets Lowcountry kick from Mustard Seed's Troy Timpner and his delectable addition of pan-seared salmon and fried green tomatoes. So don't waste any time: grab your appetite and a hefty stack of napkins and dig right in. There's no doubt the celebrated earl would if he could, poor guy.

El Bohio

1977 Maybank Highway, James Island
(843) 571-4343
www.charlestonpourhouse.com
Owners: Vanessa Luis Harris and Alex Harris

The mojo's always on the rise at this cupboard of a Cuban restaurant on James Island. Mojo, a saucy blend of fresh citrus juices, olive oil, garlic, and oregano, makes a showing in nearly every dish here, offering flavorful jolts of bona fide Cuban deliciousness. The restaurant is owned and operated by first-generation American Vanessa Luis Harris and her husband, Alex. Vanessa took cues from her mother's kitchen and childhood memories of Miami's Cuban neighborhoods to put together the rich menu of Cuban peasant staples. Dark, sweet Cuban bread, *papas rellenas,* and empanadas are delivered from a bakery in Miami, and then Vanessa works her natural magic on El Bohio's simply soulful fare.

El bohio is a Cuban term for a "humble home with sand floors and thatched roofing," according to Vanessa. True to form, her "design freak" mother transformed the tiny, fifty-seat space into just that. Cuban cigar boxes house exotic condiments on every table, and high-backed wooden booths make it easy to feel like you're in the old country.

"When it comes to cooking in Cuba," says Vanessa, "we use what's available." Citrus is prevalent in the Caribbean, so that's why it shows up in the mojo here. Vanessa's other tricks for making an idyllic Cuban sandwich are slow-roasted pork, smoked ham, excellent Swiss cheese, and, of course, Cuban bread. If you can't get it, go with the best-quality baguette you can find and prepare to dip! This is good stuff.

Cuban Sandwich

(Serves 4)

For the pulled pork:

1 3–4-pound pork shoulder
2 tablespoons ground cumin
2 tablespoons salt
2 tablespoons freshly ground black pepper

For the mojo sauce:

1 cup fresh-squeezed orange juice
1 cup fresh-squeezed lime juice
2 cups olive oil
3 tablespoons minced garlic

1 tablespoon ground cumin
1 tablespoon dried oregano leaves
1 tablespoon salt
1 tablespoon freshly ground black pepper

For the sandwiches:

1 loaf Cuban bread (or substitute a French or Italian loaf)
20 dill pickle chips
8 slices smoked ham
8 slices Swiss cheese
¼ cup yellow mustard

To prepare the pulled pork, preheat the oven to 350°F. Rub the shoulder evenly with the cumin, salt, and pepper. Place in a roasting pan, fatty side up, with ½ cup of water in the bottom. Cover tightly with foil. Roast slowly for 6 to 8 hours or until the middle bones come out easily. Remove from the oven and let cool. Once the meat is cool enough to handle, cut off the top layer of fat and discard. Pull the meat off the shoulder bone, shredding it with your fingers and discarding any extra fat. Place the meat in a pan and keep warm in a low oven, or refrigerate, tightly wrapped in foil, overnight. Bring to room temperature by setting outside the refrigerator for 2 hours. The meat will re-heat naturally during the grilling process.

Meanwhile, prepare the mojo sauce by combining all of the sauce ingredients in a medium bowl. Refrigerate at least 30 minutes and up to several hours before serving. Serve cool or at room temperature.

To assemble the sandwiches, cut the Cuban loaf into four equal parts. Slice each piece of bread lengthwise into two pieces. For each sandwich, place four or five dill pickles on the bottom half of the bread and top with two slices of smoked ham, two slices of Swiss cheese, and ¼ cup of the pulled pork. Spread the top half of the bread liberally with mustard and top the sandwich. To heat, cook the sandwiches in a sandwich press until golden and bubbly. If you do not own a sandwich press, heat a large skillet over medium-high heat and set two sandwiches at a time in it, bottom side up. Press down with a spatula or another skillet to get the pressed effect. After about 2 minutes, flip the sandwich and repeat on the other side.

At El Bohio, the sandwiches are sliced in half at an angle and served with a small ramekin of room-temperature mojo sauce.

Poe's Tavern

2210 Middle Street, Sullivan's Island
(843) 883-0083
WWW.POESTAVERN.COM
Executive Chef/Kitchen Manager: Jimmy Coste

Telltale clues of Edgar Allan Poe's life and works lurk in the many nooks of this beach bungalow, situated on the island where Poe was stationed as a U.S. Army soldier in 1827 and where he penned "The Gold Bug." Black silhouettes of Poe's tragic countenance and several ravens set a dark mood that is all at once lightened by the hipster, relaxed beach groove at Poe's. "When I look into the restaurant and it is dark and the fires are going, I think this is the kind of place Poe would enjoy. And everyone knows he enjoyed his drink," says executive chef Jimmy Coste.

Indeed, the central bamboo-topped bar is open and invites sea breezes and easy conversations, rendering Poe's very much a popular watering hole. But folks come to Poe's just as much for the restaurant's epic burgers and fish tacos as its beer. All the burgers are cleverly named for Poe stories (Pit & Pendulum, Black Cat, and, of course, Gold-Bug) and are prepared with certified Angus chuck, ground in-house and cooked to order. Jimmy, a Sullivan's Island native, insists on choice beef. "When you eat our hamburgers, you're getting meat that was ground that morning. They're so good because they're so fresh. Eating a burger here is practically like eating steak on a bun," Jimmy rightfully gushes.

Jimmy likes to shake up the burger menu with weekly burger specials. He's tried teriyaki grilled pineapple, fried pickles, black bean cakes, a Cuban burger—"You name it, we've probably tried it," he says. The Sleeper, a six-ounce burger topped with roasted garlic blue cheese and fried buffalo shrimp, was a special that was so revered it earned a permanent spot on Poe's menu.

The Sleeper
(Serves 6)

For the garlic blue cheese sauce:

¼ cup garlic cloves (about 8 cloves)
1 tablespoon olive oil
1 pound blue cheese, coarsely crumbled
¾ cup mayonnaise
Salt and freshly ground black pepper to taste

For the burgers:

2 pounds plus 4 ounces freshly ground certified Angus choice chuck beef (ask your butcher to grind the beef to your specifications when you purchase it)
Salt and freshly ground pepper to taste

For the buffalo fried shrimp:

2 cups milk
1 egg
Salt and freshly ground black pepper to taste
2 cups flour
1 tablespoon Old Bay Seasoning
30–36 medium shrimp, peeled and deveined,
    tails removed
3 cups peanut oil
1 cup Texas Pete Mild Chicken Wing Sauce
    (or Hot Chicken Wing Sauce, if desired)

To serve:

6 high-quality hamburger buns (Poe's are made
    by a local bakery)

Prepare the garlic blue cheese sauce up to 3 days in advance. Preheat the oven to 375°F. Line up the garlic cloves on a small roasting pan and drizzle with olive oil. Cover tightly with aluminum foil. Roast until golden brown, about 30 minutes. Set aside to cool. When cooled, blend garlic in the bowl of a food processor until smooth. Transfer the garlic puree to a medium bowl and combine, stirring gently, with the blue cheese, mayonnaise, and salt and pepper to taste. Cover and refrigerate until ready to use.

Meanwhile, form the hamburger into six 6-ounce patties. Season the exteriors lightly with salt and pepper. Cover with plastic wrap and refrigerate up to 12 hours before cooking.

To prepare the fried shrimp, combine the milk, egg, and salt and pepper to taste in a shallow bowl, mixing well with a fork. Separately, combine the flour, Old Bay Seasoning, and salt and pepper to taste in a second shallow bowl, mixing well with a fork. To bread the shrimp, first dip in the flour mixture, tapping off any excess, then dip in the

milk and egg mixture, then finish by dipping in the flour mixture again. Be sure to tap off any excess flour. Set shrimp aside.

Just before serving, heat the peanut oil in a medium saucepan over medium heat until it reaches 325°F to 350°F. In the meantime, cook the burgers on a grill or in a large sauté pan over medium or medium-high heat to desired doneness. Remove and set aside, keeping warm. When the oil is hot, fry the shrimp in batches until they are golden brown, about 2 minutes. Remove with a slotted spoon and drain over paper towels. When cool enough to handle, toss the shrimp with the hot sauce in a medium bowl. To serve, place each burger on a bun and top with about ¼ cup of the garlic blue cheese sauce. Top with five or six warm Buffalo Shrimp. Serve immediately and pass the napkins!

Jack's Cosmic Dogs

2805 Highway 17 North, Mount Pleasant
(843) 884-7677
WWW.JACKSCOSMICDOGS.COM
Owner: Jack Hurley

After graduating from the College of William & Mary with a business degree in 1972, Jack Hurley decided he was "done being told what to do." So he put together his own "bucket list" and hitchhiked, skied, took a train across the Rockies, met his wife, and otherwise played until he turned twenty-seven. That year, the maverick who calls himself "Big Dog" discovered his trade and opened his first restaurant in Burlington, Vermont. Many moons and several successful restaurants and businesses later, the Big Dog still barks with joy as the top dog at Jack's Cosmic Dogs, a hip hot dog joint that combines Jack's love for all things quirky and cosmic and wraps it all up in an oversized Pepperidge Farm bun.

A Flash Gordonesque model rocket, moon pies, cream sodas, a 1950s-style cooler, and a red Sunbeam white bread sign give Cosmic Jack's a comforting blast-from-the-past feel with a new age twist. Throw in 98 percent beef (the remaining 2 percent is pork) Boar's Head dogs and a smattering of original condiments from Jack's repertoire, and it's no surprise that Jack's got kids of all ages bow-wowing for more.

Tangy blue cheese slaw and Jack's jarred sweet potato mustard (available for purchase on his Web site) dress up Jack's signature cosmic dog. The sweet heat from the mustard is the perfect foil for the mellow bite of blue cheese and the crunch of the slaw and is part of what makes this dog so hot-diggedy-dog delicious. Meanwhile, there's no reason for vegetarians to skip this party: the "Vegaroid" Dog features Morningstar tofu dogs slathered with yellow mustard, ketchup, and onions.

Jack's Cosmic Dog
(Serves 6)

For the blue cheese slaw:

1 small head green cabbage, finely sliced
¼ small head red cabbage, finely sliced
1 carrot, peeled and finely sliced
1 cup sour cream
1 cup mayonnaise
1½ teaspoons garlic powder
½ teaspoon dried oregano
½ teaspoon onion powder
½ cup crumbled high-quality blue cheese
Salt and freshly ground black pepper to taste

For the hot dogs:

6 Boar's Head hot dogs (Jack also recommends Hebrew National hot dogs)
6 Pepperidge Farm oversized hot dog buns
¼ cup Jack's Sweet Potato Mustard

Up to 2 hours before serving, combine all of the slaw ingredients in a large bowl, stirring well to combine. Taste and adjust seasoning as needed. Cover and reserve at room temperature.

Steam or grill the hot dogs according to package directions. To assemble the hot dogs, spread a generous tablespoon of Jack's Sweet Potato Mustard on both sides of the inside of each bun. Top the mustard-swathed buns with the warm hot dogs and about ¼ cup of the slaw. Serve immediately. At Jack's, the dogs come with a cone of sweet potato French fries.

FIVE LOAVES CAFÉ

43 CANNON STREET, DOWNTOWN
(843) 397-4303
1055 JOHNNIE DODDS BOULEVARD, SUITE 50, MOUNT PLEASANT
(843) 849-1043
WWW.FIVELOAVESCAFE.COM
EXECUTIVE CHEF/CO-OWNER: CASEY GLOWACKI

Not even divorce, a beloved dog's death, jury duty, and excruciating back pain could deter tenacious chef Casey Glowacki (see Sesame Burgers & Beer, page 96) from achieving his dream and opening his first restaurant, Five Loaves Café (downtown). Unbelievably, all those nasty things converged during the restaurant's early days, back in 2003. Not only did the restaurant survive, it thrives as the "great little soup and sandwich shop" he and his business partner, Joe Fischbein, envisioned. Unlike the original plan, however, demand for Casey's soup was so hot that the menu was expanded to include dinner and, later, a second location in Mount Pleasant.

A disciple of revered restaurant maven Sal Parco (of the Mustard Seed Restaurant Group; see Uno Mas, page 16, and Mustard Seed, page 100), Casey's tenure with Sal provided him with the experience, confidence, and coin to finance the venture. Five Loaves teems with bohemian energy and garden-fresh goodness. Sandwiches are served on six mix-and-match varieties of bread made daily at a local bakery. Casey still gets busy in the kitchen, where he indulges in his preferred passion—making soup. "I think a good soup is the biggest proof of a good chef," he says. Robin-egg blue benches make for comfortable perches, and quotations from artists and authors inlaid in each table make for witty reading while savoring Glowacki's goods.

This yummy vegetarian sandwich, one of many vegetarian offerings at the restaurants, is a rendition of a recipe that Casey prepared at a deli and gourmet market he once worked at in Telluride, Colorado. It tastes just as good in Charleston.

Roasted Portobello Sandwich with Sweet Onion, Roasted Red Pepper, and Parmesan Spinach Spread

(Serves 6)

For the mushrooms:

6 whole portobello mushrooms, stems removed
4 tablespoons chopped garlic
2 tablespoons olive oil
Salt and freshly ground black pepper to taste

For the sweet onions:

1 tablespoon olive oil
1 onion, finely sliced
Salt and freshly ground black pepper to taste

For the roasted red peppers:

2 red bell peppers

For the Parmesan spinach spread:

1 cup grated sharp cheddar cheese
2 cups grated Parmesan cheese
¼ cup mayonnaise
2 cups fresh spinach, tough stems removed
Salt and freshly ground black pepper to taste

For the sandwiches:

12 thick slices high-quality whole-grain bread
   (or substitute preferred bread type)
1 large tomato, thinly sliced
1½ cups fresh mesclun

To prepare the mushrooms, preheat the oven to 375°F. Gently rub the garlic into the rib-side (interior) of the mushroom caps. Lay caps rib-side up on a sheet pan and drizzle with olive oil, salt, and pepper. Roast for 12 minutes. Set aside to cool.

Meanwhile, prepare the onions. Heat the olive oil over medium heat in a medium sauté pan. Add the onion, season with salt and pepper, and cook until the onions take on a golden color and are very soft, about 12 minutes. Set aside.

Roast the peppers over an open gas flame on the stovetop, turning occasionally to blacken the entire surface of each pepper. (The peppers can also be roasted under the broiler or purchased prepared.) Rinse the roasted peppers under a steady stream of cold water, removing the blackened skin, ribs, and seeds. Chop the roasted pepper into coarse strips and set aside.

Prepare the Parmesan spinach spread by combining the cheddar, Parmesan, mayonnaise, fresh spinach, and salt and pepper in the bowl of a food processor. Blend until chunky-smooth. Adjust seasoning as needed.

To assemble the sandwiches, line up the bread slices on your working surface. Spread one side of each slice with Parmesan spinach spread. Top six of the slices with about ¼ cup of mesclun and 2 tomato slices. Top with 1 roasted portobello cap and a portion of the sweet onions and roasted pepper. Top with the remaining slices of bread. Serve immediately.

Sesame Burgers & Beer

4726 Spruill Avenue, North Charleston
(843) 554-4903
Executive Chef/Co-Owner: Casey Glowacki

It's in the condiments at Sesame, where young professionals and working class blokes open their minds and their mouths to the old-fashioned goodness of 100 percent house-made condiments and gourmet burgers. The latest brainchild of the enterprising Mr. Glowacki (see Five Loaves Café, page 94), Sesame produces its own pickles, mayonnaise, ketchup, sauces, and salad dressings to top what Casey refers to as a "labor-intensive menu" of burgers, sandwiches, salads, and sweets.

Located smack dab in the center of Charleston's industrial hub (referred to by locals as North Chuck), Sesame attracts a wide cast of characters (including quasi-regular North Charleston mayor Keith Summey) in search of gourmet comfort food at nice prices. Sesame offers beef, chicken, turkey, and black bean burgers with a bevy of toppings—like roasted beets and fried eggs on the New Zealander and blue cheese and fresh basil on the Italian. "People really like choices and freedom in what they eat and if you don't give them just that, they walk," says Casey.

No wonder locals run to Sesame. A signature staple here is the Ultimate Grilled Cheese, a sultry blend of nutty Tillamook cheddar, tangy Brie, and smooth, gooey Fontina melted between a layer of tomatoes and thick sourdough bread. What's the condiment of choice for this beauty? House-made aioli. Who knew grilled cheese could be so heavenly?

Ultimate Grilled Cheese with Tillamook Cheddar, Brie, and Fontina with Tomatoes and Garlic Aioli on Sourdough

(Serves 4)

For the aioli:

1 head garlic
1 large egg
1 tablespoon Dijon mustard
Juice of 1 lemon
2 tablespoons rice wine vinegar
Salt and freshly ground black pepper to taste
1 cup canola oil
1 cup olive oil

For the sandwiches:

8 thick slices sourdough bread
6 ounces Tillamook cheddar, sliced
4 ounces Brie, sliced
4 ounces Fontina cheese, sliced
1 large tomato, sliced
4 tablespoons butter

Preheat the oven to 375°F. Wrap the head of garlic tightly in aluminum foil. Roast until soft, about 40 minutes, and remove from the oven. Once garlic is cool enough to handle, squeeze the pulp out of the casing of 4 cloves, reserving the remaining garlic for another use. (The remaining roasted garlic pulp can be stored in the refrigerator in a small covered container for use in salad dressings or additional aioli or to top roasted meats.)

To prepare the aioli, place the 4 cloves of garlic in the bowl of a food processor with the remaining aioli ingredients, except the oils. Puree until smooth. Gradually, through the tube of the food processor, drizzle in the olive and canola oils in a slow and steady stream. (The aioli should initially be thick and then take on the appearance and texture of mayonnaise. Be patient streaming in the oil. The binders in the mayonnaise need time to absorb the oil. If it breaks and looks oily and ugly, remove the contents from the bowl and clean it thoroughly. Reserve the broken mayonnaise. Add another egg yolk and a

tablespoon of mustard to the cleaned bowl, pulse together, and gradually incorporate the broken aioli in a steady stream. This should repair it!) Taste and adjust salt and pepper as needed.

To assemble the sandwiches, line up the bread slices on a clean work surface. Spread each slice with a generous layer (about 1 tablespoon) of aioli. (Refrigerate leftover aioli for future sandwiches, but be sure to use it within a few days, as it is perishable.) Layer 4 of the slices with each of the cheeses and top with 2 slices of tomato. Top each sandwich with the remaining pieces of bread. Heat a griddle or two large sauté pans over medium heat. Distribute the butter evenly among the pans and melt. Place the sandwiches on the warmed griddle or pans when the butter is bubbling. Heat until golden brown on the first side, about 4 minutes. Flip sandwiches and repeat on the second side. Casey says "the cheese should be hot and melted and the bread should not be burned." Patience and an eagle eye on the grill are the keys to success here!

GAULART & MALICLET

98 BROAD STREET, DOWNTOWN
(843) 577-9797
WWW.FASTANDFRENCH.ORG
WORKING OWNERS: GWYLENE GALLIMARD AND JEAN-MARIE MAUCLET

You won't be served a Coca-Cola or any kind of soft drink to wash down your *chien chaud* at this endearing French cafe, more commonly referred to as Fast & French. That's because Parisian native Gwylene Gallimard doesn't believe in clobbering good food with the cloying sweetness of Coke. "We serve wine to balance the food. It should not overpower the food, but complement it," she says. Water, microbrewed beers, and sweet tea are alternative choices to pair with the cafe's myriad soup and sandwich lunch combinations and *tres* French dinner menu, composed of bouillabaisse, house-made fondue, escargot, and couscous.

Jean-Marie Mauclet, Gwylene's partner in life and business, grew up in his grandfather's cafe and his mother's kitchen in northern France and is the creative genius behind nearly all of the tantalizingly French, yet homey recipes that have been dished out here for a quarter of a century. Folks return time and again for the relaxed Francophile environs and the bohemian buzz created by the scent of rich coffee and the quiet banter of the mostly black-clad guests.

At the restaurant, this spunky sandwich is served warm and made to order. Make a big batch of the tapenade—this recipe makes enough for about twenty sandwiches—and save the leftovers to serve as an appetizer with cheese and wine. The tapenade will store for several days in the refrigerator. Bon appétit!

SANDWICH PROVENÇALE
(Makes 1 sandwich)

For the tapenade:

2½ cups pitted olives (green or black niçoise), coarsely chopped
1¼ cups extra-virgin olive oil
2½ green bell peppers, seeded and cut into quarters
2 large tomatoes, cored and coarsely chopped
1 medium zucchini, peeled and coarsely chopped
½ cup coarsely chopped fresh parsley
1 tablespoon fresh-squeezed lemon juice, or to taste
6 cloves fresh garlic, coarsely chopped
1 tablespoon freshly ground black pepper
Salt to taste

For the sandwich:

¼ of a high-quality fresh baguette, sliced lengthwise
1 ounce fresh goat cheese
2 slices fresh tomato
2 teaspoons chopped fresh basil

Taste the olives you're using for the tapenade before you get started. If they're extra salty, rinse them to remove excess salt, and keep their salt content in mind as you're seasoning. To prepare the tapenade, combine all the tapenade ingredients in the bowl of a food processor and pulse together until the consistency is medium-fine. You want the pieces to be about one-quarter the size of a pea. Taste and adjust seasoning as necessary. (The tapenade can be prepared several days in advance and stored in the refrigerator. For the best flavor, use the tapenade at room temperature.)

To assemble the sandwich, preheat the broiler or a toaster oven to high. Spread one half of the sliced baguette with goat cheese. Place both halves of the baguette, cut side up, under the broiler or in the toaster oven and toast until the bread is crisp and golden and the cheese has softened. Evenly spread the tapenade on the bare half of the sandwich and top this with the tomato slices. Sprinkle the goat cheese half with the fresh basil. Serve immediately, either open-faced or closed.

Mustard Seed

1970 Maybank Highway, James Island
(843) 762-0072
1036 Chuck Dawley Boulevard, Mount Pleasant
(843) 849-0050
101 North Main Street, Summerville
(843) 721-7101
WWW.DINEWITHSAL.COM
Director of Culinary Directions: William "Troy" Timpner

Chain restaurants and franchises aside, Sal Parco, owner of these restaurants and five other local eateries, is hands-down greater Charleston's most prolific restaurateur. His first restaurant here was the original Mustard Seed in Mount Pleasant, but now, like seeds awakening to the warmth of spring, Mustard Seed has sprung to include two additional restaurants with the same vegetarian, seafood, and reasonably priced themes.

The biggest and most heavily trafficked restaurant is far and away the James Island location—a spacious, casual spot with the added bonus of plentiful free parking. Troy Timpner oversees all three of the restaurants with a firm but fair attitude and an eye toward freshness. The no-nonsense Destin, Florida, native takes special pride in the specials board, which features up to ten snappy items daily, in addition to the substantial menu. "I don't want our clients to see the same thing this week that they saw last week," Troy says. At Mustard Seed, popular specials like Troy's spectacular Salmon and Fried Green Tomato BLT evolve into permanent menu items. This may well become one in your house! (To save time, feel free to substitute store-bought focaccia.)

Mustard Seed Salmon and Fried Green Tomato BLT
(Serves 4)

For the focaccia:

6 tablespoons warm water (at body temperature)
1½ teaspoons active dry yeast
2 tablespoons sugar
2 cups bread flour
1½ teaspoons plus 4 tablespoons extra-virgin olive oil
2 teaspoons salt
1 tablespoon dried basil
½ cup finely grated Parmesan cheese

For the sun-dried tomato pesto:

½ cup sun-dried tomatoes
2 cloves garlic
¼ cup fresh basil
¼ cup walnuts
¼ cup grated Parmesan cheese
½ cup olive oil
Salt and freshly ground black pepper to taste
1 cup mayonnaise

For the fried green tomatoes:

2 cups panko bread crumbs
½ cup grated Parmesan cheese
2 cups buttermilk
2 cups flour
Salt and freshly ground black pepper to taste
¼ cup peanut oil
8 thick slices green tomatoes

For the sandwiches:

1 tablespoon olive oil
4 6-ounce salmon fillets
Salt and freshly ground black pepper to taste
8 slices applewood-smoked bacon
1 cup mixed fresh greens
½ red onion, thinly sliced

Begin by making the focaccia. Preheat the oven
to 450°F. In a large mixer bowl, combine the water,
yeast, and sugar. Allow the yeast to "bloom" (proof)
for about 5 minutes or until the surface is bubbly.
Add the flour, 1½ teaspoons olive oil, 1 teaspoon
salt, and the basil. Using the mixer's dough hook or
pastry arm, mix the dough on low until it forms a ball
and has a doughy consistency, about 2 minutes.
Continue mixing on medium for 8 to 10 minutes.
Cover the dough in the bowl with plastic wrap.
Allow the dough to rise until doubled in size, about
1 hour. Punch down the dough on a lightly greased
9 x 13-inch sheet pan. Cover and allow the dough
to rise again, for about 30 minutes. Using your
fingertips, press the dough down and pull it gently
so that it extends to the edges of the pan. Leave
the dimples created by your fingertips. Drizzle the
dough with the remaining 4 tablespoons olive oil,
the remaining 1 teaspoon salt, and the Parmesan
cheese. Preheat the oven to 450°F. Bake for 20
minutes, rotating it 180-degree in the pan halfway
through the baking time. Remove the bread from
the oven and set aside.

To prepare the sun-dried tomato pesto, rehydrate the dried tomatoes in ½ cup of warm water. Set aside for about an hour. After the tomatoes are rehydrated, pour off any excess water and combine the tomatoes with the garlic, basil, walnuts, Parmesan cheese, olive oil, and salt and pepper in the bowl of a food processor. Puree until smooth. Turn out the pesto into a medium bowl and combine with the mayonnaise until blended. Cover and reserve. (The pesto can be prepared a day or two in advance.)

To prepare the tomatoes, combine the panko bread crumbs and the Parmesan in a shallow bowl. Pour the buttermilk into another shallow bowl. Season the flour lightly with salt and pepper and place it in a third shallow bowl. Heat a large sauté pan over medium-high heat. Once the pan is warmed, pour in the oil and get it just-bubbling-hot when the oil begins to move and swivel in the pan over medium-high heat. Dip each tomato slice first in the flour (tap off excess), then in the buttermilk, and then in the bread crumb mixture (tap off excess). Put the tomato slices in the pan, being careful not to crowd (do in two batches if necessary), and brown on the first side (about 2 minutes), then flip and repeat on the second side. Drain on paper towels and season lightly with salt and pepper, if desired.

Get ready to assemble the sandwiches. Heat the olive oil in a medium sauté pan over medium-high heat. Season the salmon lightly on both sides with salt and pepper. Cook a few minutes on each side, turning when browned, to desired doneness. Remove pan from the heat. Meanwhile, cook the bacon over medium-high heat in a large sauté pan. Drain the bacon on paper towels. Cut four 4-inch-thick slices from the focaccia and cut each in half horizontally. Arrange four of the bottom halves on your work surface. Spread each with a few tablespoons of the pesto. Top with about ¼ cup fresh greens and a few slivers of onion. Next, add the warm salmon, and top each piece with two slices of bacon. Replace the sandwich tops and serve immediately.

"JESUS CRAB" AND DIVINE FRIED SEAFOOD

Becky and Joe Pleasants opened this dive of a road-side find—situated near the turn-off to the tony island resorts of Kiawah and Seabrook—to sell some of Joe's excess crab and seafood he snared as a commercial crabber. He's still crabbing and fishing, but in the ten years since opening, Becky and her small kitchen crew at Fishnet Seafood have mastered the elusive art of fried seafood, from whiting to shrimp to "Jesus crab"—so called because the couple's autistic son thought it righteous to "drive the devil out" of the deviled crab with the goodwill (and good name) of Jesus.

Fishnet sticks with 100 percent peanut oil for frying and serves only fresh-off-the-boat seafood. All items are breaded and fried to order, including soft-shell crabs dipped in a combo of House-Autry and Atkinson's brand "breader," served on white bread and topped with hot garlic butter. Yellow corn flour provides the special crunch for the crab and all the fried seafood, but Becky declined to share any more details of her secret recipes.

She did offer the simple recipe for the garlic butter that dresses the not-to-be-missed soft-shell crab sandwich. She combines ¼ cup garlic powder with ¼ cup Old Bay Seasoning and brings it to a boil with 5 pounds of butter for "about 27 minutes." Try your luck at home, or better yet, when in town, swing on by and visit the old gas station turned fabulous fried seafood shack at 3832 Savannah Highway, just past the turn-off to Johns Island on the western cusp of West Ashley and Johns Island. Call ahead for orders: (843) 571-2423.

Mondo's

915 Folly Road, James Island
(843) 795-8400
www.eatatmondos.com
Owner/Chef: Chris Orlando

Fresh out of cooking school (Johnson & Wales) and with just $300 in their respective pockets on opening night in 1998, Chris Orlando and former partner Josh Montalto combined youthful early-twenties enthusiasm and their last names to create Mondo's. The original plan was to operate a deli, but with time and increased customer demand, Mondo's morphed into what it is today, a kind of everyman culinary hot spot, serving everything from pasta, fish, and soup to sandwiches, well over a decade into its winning season.

Chris is from South Philly, an area of town with a heavy Italian concentration. He grew up watching his grandfather, a tailor by trade, cook. All of this heavily influenced his penchant for what he calls "Italian soul food." But don't be surprised by Mondo's hefty concentration of Southern flair and use of locally grown produce and seafood. "If we have good local oysters, I might throw them into the risotto. I use what's around me and what's fresh, but my roots are really what I've grown up on," he adds.

Chris humbly credits word-of-mouth advertising, gentle prices, and an exceptionally loyal clientele with Mondo's success. But there's a reason for all that warm buzz—great food. Chris remembers sitting on the washer in his grandparents' basement kitchen and watching his grandfather roast and shave pork. "It's something he made and it's something I do every day, just the way he taught me," he says. This sandwich is the restaurant's third-best seller and one sandwich in which Chris takes obvious and deserved pride.

Mondo's Italian Pork Roast Sandwich
(Serves 6)

For the pork:

1½–2 pounds pork loin, trimmed of extra sinew
    and fat
4 tablespoons finely chopped fresh rosemary
8 garlic cloves, finely minced
Kosher salt and freshly ground black pepper
¼ cup olive oil

For the sandwiches:

6 hoagie rolls or mini baguettes
2 roasted peppers (see page 95), juices reserved,
    or 1½ cups prepared roasted peppers, sliced
    into ¼-inch-thick strips
3 cups fresh baby spinach
Kosher salt and freshly ground black pepper
    to taste
12 slices sharp aged provolone

To prepare the pork, preheat the oven to 350°F. Place the pork in a heavy roasting pan and pierce the top of the loin, about ½-inch deep, six to eight times with a paring knife. Combine the rosemary and garlic in a small bowl to form a rub, and rub the mixture all over the pork. Season liberally with salt and pepper. Drizzle the olive oil over the top of the pork and rub in with your hands. Roast the pork until the internal temperature reaches 145°F, 45 minutes to 1 hour, depending on the size of the roast. Let rest at room temperature for 20 minutes. Reserve some of the pan juices, but skim off any excess oil and discard.

If desired, place the hoagie rolls in the warm oven until warmed through. Once the pork has rested, slice very thin or shave with a sharp knife or meat slicer. Combine the reserved pepper juices (or the juice from a can or jar of prepared peppers, if using) with the pan juices from the pork and bring to a simmer in a large sauté pan over medium-high heat. Add the pepper strips, spinach, and about 6 cups of the pork (you will have some left over). Stir to combine and heat through. Season to taste with salt and pepper.

To assemble the sandwiches, fill each hoagie with equal parts of the pork mixture. Top each with 2 slices of provolone. The cheese will melt with the heat of the filling. Serve immediately.

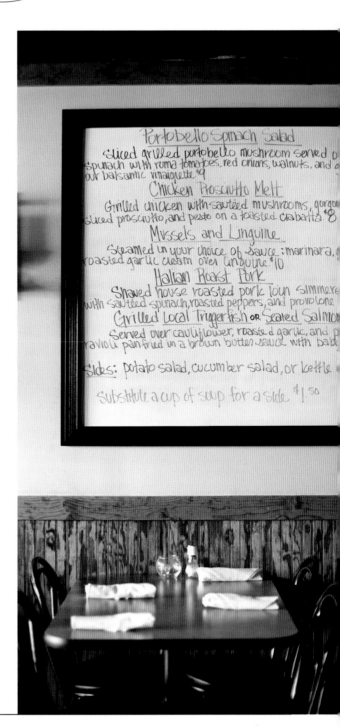

PALMETTO CAFÉ

205 MEETING STREET (AT CHARLESTON PLACE), DOWNTOWN
(843) 722-4900
WWW.CHARLESTONPLACE.COM
CHEF DE CUISINE: STUART TRACY

Seek out the hushed, plush confines of casually sophisticated Palmetto Café whenever a mild indulgence or a heady business lunch is in order. The courtyard's verdant flora and the steady gurgle of a tall fountain create the consummate secret garden. Deep and well-cushioned chairs complete the comfort scene, and then there's the food.

Chef de cuisine Stuart Tracy came to Charleston to attend Johnson & Wales and stayed to commence a noteworthy career, working with the likes of Ken Vedrinski (see Trattoria Lucca, page 112) and other talents of equal stature. "Working with Ken, I really came to appreciate how good food is when it's prepared the old-fashioned way with pristine ingredients," says Stuart.

He puts his knowledge and passion to play at Palmetto Café with "new twists on old favorites," like ham and cheese, peanut butter and jelly, and fish and chips. Of all the fancy dishes he's prepared, sandwiches are one of his favorite things to create because there's no limit to the combinations of bread or fillings. An admitted sucker for a great burger (and the 21 burger here is a sumptuous treat), Stuart's Seafood Club Sandwich pays homage to his yen for new interpretations of old classics. A play on the classic club, this tower of elegance and taste features smoked salmon, smoked salmon spread, shrimp, Maine lobster, and a warm béarnaise sauce.

PALMETTO CAFÉ SEAFOOD CLUB SANDWICH
(Serves 4)

For the salmon spread:

⅓ cup coarsely chopped smoked salmon
¼ cup crème fraîche or sour cream
1 tablespoon fresh-squeezed lemon juice
Salt to taste
Tabasco sauce to taste

For the béarnaise:

2 sticks (½ pound) unsalted butter, melted
3 tablespoons white wine
3 tablespoons white vinegar
2 tablespoons finely chopped shallots
1 tablespoon finely chopped fresh tarragon leaves
3 egg yolks

2 tablespoons water
Salt to taste
Tabasco sauce to taste

For the sandwiches:

12 slices Pullman-style (square) white bread
16 slices smoked salmon
16 slices applewood-smoked bacon, cooked
3 to 4 Roma tomatoes, cut into 24 thin slices
1–1½ cups fresh arugula, micro greens,
    or mesclun
12 South Carolina extra-large (16–20 count)
    white shrimp, cooked, peeled and deveined
2 Maine lobster tails, cooked, shelled and
    halved horizontally

To make the salmon spread, combine all ingredients in a food processor and puree until smooth. Taste and adjust seasoning as necessary. Set aside or refrigerate in a sealed container if you will not be using within 30 minutes. The spread can be made 1 or 2 days in advance and refrigerated until ready to use.

Because a béarnaise can be persnickety if kept warm very long, prep the other sandwich ingredients first, then make the sauce just before you assemble the sandwiches. To prepare the béarnaise, prepare the clarified butter. Next, combine the wine, vinegar, and shallots in a small saucepan and cook over medium-high heat until the liquid has cooked down to a glaze. In a glass or stainless steel bowl over a gently simmering water bath or double boiler, vigorously whisk together the egg yolks and water until thick ribbons appear when you pull the whisk away, 2 or 3 minutes. Scrape the bottom of the bowl every so often to avoid scrambling the eggs. The eggs should be at about body temperature. Remove the bowl from the heat and slowly stream in the warm clarified butter, whisking to combine. Add the shallot mixture and tarragon, and season to taste with salt and Tabasco. Serve within 10 minutes or so, or return the bowl to the top of the warm water bath, with the heat turned off.

To assemble the sandwiches, stack the bread and cut off the crusts with a bread knife. Slice an additional 2 inches off one side of each piece of bread so the square will become a rectangle. (Use the discarded bread for bread crumbs.)

Each sandwich is composed of three layers. The top layer (do this first) is not toasted and is spread with 1 tablespoon salmon spread and 4 slices of smoked salmon. Trim off any salmon that overlaps the borders.

Toast the remaining bread lightly (either under the broiler or in a toaster) and then arrange the middle and bottom layers. The middle layer is composed of a slice of toasted bread, spread with 1 teaspoon salmon spread, and topped with 2 slices bacon, 3 slices of tomato, a sprinkling of greens, and 3 cooked shrimp. The bottom layer is composed of a slice of toasted bread, spread with 1 teaspoon salmon spread, and topped with 2 slices bacon, 3 slices of tomato, a sprinkling of greens, and half a cooked lobster tail.

Stack the sandwich layers and serve each sandwich with a small ramekin of warm béarnaise sauce.

Pasta

We're knee-deep in noodles and deep-seated Latin passion for food and cooking in this chapter, twirling and swirling with the delights of pappardelle, ravioli, risotto (a kind of Italian rice), and more. The chefs and restaurants featured here share more than pasta in common. All have blood ties to the old country and all but one are relative newcomers to the Charleston Italian restaurant scene, a reflection of the unequaled growth this restaurant category has experienced here in recent years.

This is an impassioned bunch! Most of these chefs grew up cooking with their Italian grandmothers or grandfathers and all speak of the importance of simplicity, freshness, technique, and love in cooking.

Regardless of its shape or whether the pasta is fresh or dry, the key to show-stopping pasta dishes is the sauce. Amuse's James "Doc" Trez's unbelievable Bolognese gets a pinch of French classical technique and has a huge splash of sweet slow-cooked flavor that wraps around each strand of soothing spaghetti, sending happiness straight to your heart. Lucca's Ken Vedrinski takes Tuscan inspiration and his Italian Grandmother Volpe's ragu to task over hand-rolled ricotta gnudi, while Vinny Lombardi delivers Brooklyn to Charleston with an endless supply of "gravy" and chef Rick Agius's Sweet Potato Ravioli with Sage Brown Butter Sauce, Walnuts, and Gorgonzola. Travel once again to Tuscany and Pane e Vino's Massimiliano Sarrocchi's childhood boar hunting memories with Massi's smashing Wild Boar Stew with Pappardelle.

Remember, when cooking pasta, the water needs to be well salted, as salty as sea water, in fact. Count on about 3 to 4 tablespoons per half gallon.

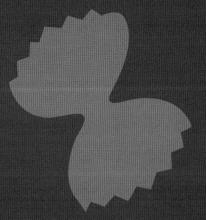

Amuse Restaurant

1720 Sam Rittenberg Boulevard, West Ashley
(843) 573-8778
www.amuserestaurant.net
Executive Chef/Owner: James "Doc" Trez

Even though he discovered an early passion (a word he uses convincingly and frequently) for cooking and had spent time working in professional kitchens since he was twelve, the tragedy of 9/11 got Doc Trez thinking about enlisting in the army. But it was the inspirational beauty of a family trip to Napa a few weeks later that persuaded him food was his destiny. So when he returned to Charleston, he responded to an ad in the paper for a sous chef at a new small Italian restaurant and, as the forty-fifth candidate interviewed for the job, got the gig.

The "small Italian restaurant" turned out to be a huge, heaven-sent wonderland of Italian goodness called Al di La. Doc speaks of the two years he spent there with obvious appreciation for everything he learned under John Marshall. "We shared the same views on just about everything, especially how much it meant to us both to take care of people with good food," he says.

Still, all good things must come to an end, and in 2004, Doc opened Amuse as a tapas bar with his brother Joe and his parents. Joe's moved on to other ventures, but Amuse remains the wonderful West Ashley gem it's always been. These days it's infused with Doc's Italian-born grandmother's legacy and her 100-year-old recipe book. Doc introduced some of the dishes to the menu a few years ago as a kind of ode to her following her death. "Nonna used to always say cooking is in your heart and in your hands and that only some people are born with it," says Doc.

There's no question he was, and the proof is in this spot-on, slightly sweet and classic interpretation of a Bolognese sauce. "The most important thing about a Bolognese is to remember that it's a sauce made with meat and tomatoes, not one made mostly with tomatoes and some meat," Doc explains. He serves it over fresh spaghetti prepared by local noodle master Brian Bertolini, of Rio Bertolini's Pasta, but dry spaghetti will do. This is a beauty of a sauce. You'll be returning to this recipe again and again for more.

Spaghetti Bolognese
(Serves 6)

¼ cup olive oil
1½ pounds ground veal
1½ pounds ground pork
1½ pounds ground beef
Salt and freshly ground black pepper to taste
1 cup finely chopped onion
½ cup finely chopped peeled carrots
½ cup finely chopped celery

2 cups tomato puree
¼ cup finely chopped fresh rosemary, plus more for garnish (optional)
¼ cup finely chopped fresh sage, plus more for garnish (optional)
2 tablespoons finely chopped garlic
1 pound dried spaghetti

Heat a large saucepan or Dutch oven over medium heat. Add the olive oil, covering the bottom of the pan. Add the veal, pork, and beef. Cook, covered, and occasionally stirring, steaming the meat, but being careful not to brown it or allow it to stick to the bottom of the pan, for 12 to 15 minutes. Season lightly with salt and pepper. Add the onion, carrots, and celery and continue cooking until the vegetables are softened and the meat is cooked through, another 8 to 10 minutes. Increase the heat to medium-high, add the tomatoes, and cook for 15 minutes. (The sauce should be orange at this point.) Add the rosemary, sage, and garlic, and stir to combine. The heat of the sauce will cook the garlic. Puree sauce slightly in the pot with a handheld blender. Add salt and pepper carefully to taste, cover, and keep warm over low heat.

Meanwhile, bring a large pot of cold, generously salted water to a boil over high heat. When rapidly boiling, add the pasta all at once and stir. Cook according to package directions, then drain well in a colander. Return the pasta to the pot, over medium heat, and ladle the desired amount of sauce over it. Stir to coat the pasta with the sauce. Serve on individual plates or on a platter garnished with fresh rosemary and sage, if desired.

TRATTORIA LUCCA

41 BOGARD AT THE CORNER OF ASHE, DOWNTOWN
(843) 973-3323
WWW.TRATTORIALUCCADINING.COM
CHEF/OWNER: KEN VEDRINSKI

This highly decorated celebrity chef (he's garnered three AAA Four Diamond Awards and kudos from *Esquire* and the *New York Times* at previous posts) describes the food at his latest success, a neighborhood trattoria in the largely residential, rarely-traveled-by-tourists Elliotborough area, as "real."

It is very real, replete with the intimacy, mood, and flavors of the small walled town of Lucca nestled in the rolling hills of Tuscany. "It is just like what you would find in Lucca. There is a restaurant like this just outside the walled part of the city where locals go and the tourists do not," Vedrinski says.

It's the same sapid story here, where college kids, foodie types, and professionals of every class, race, and creed converge to sup on Vedrinski's authentic Tuscan offerings, from antipasti to strozzapreti, in the cozy-yet-sophisticated confines of the hugely inviting space.

Lucca's Sheep's Milk Ricotta Gnudi ("naked pasta") combines Italian duck sausage and Vedrinski's Grandma Volpe's beef spare rib–infused tomato ragu to create ambrosia in a bowl. Scamorza cheese is a fresh or smoked cheese that is similar to mozzarella. If you can't find the former, substitute the latter. If this recipe looks daunting, keep in mind that you can save a lot of time and trouble by using prepared duck sausage and store-bought ricotta or good-quality commercial gnocchi with similar results. It just won't be exactly Grandma Volpe's way!

Sheep's Milk Ricotta Gnudi, House-Made Italian Duck Sausage, Grandma Volpe's Tomato Ragu, and Scamorza Cheese

(Serves 6)

For the ragu:

2 tablespoons olive oil
2 pounds beef spare ribs
Salt and freshly ground black pepper
1 sweet onion, finely chopped
1 clove garlic, sliced
Pinch of red pepper flakes
2 bay leaves
2 28-ounce cans whole tomatoes, drained and
    crushed by squeezing between your palm and
    fingers
½ cup coarsely chopped Parmesan cheese rinds
    (see Bacco's Parmesan broth, page 120)

For the duck sausage:

1 pound duck legs
1 tablespoon Italian seasoning (a spice blend
    containing tarragon, sage, basil, marjoram,
    savory, rosemary, and thyme)
1 tablespoon olive oil

For the ricotta gnudi:

½ gallon whole milk
¼ cup white vinegar
¼ cup sifted pastry flour or all-purpose flour
1 egg, beaten
1 cup grated aged pecorino cheese

To finish:

1 tablespoon butter
Salt and freshly ground black pepper
½ cup cubed fresh Scamorza cheese or
    fresh mozzarella
2 tablespoons chopped fresh basil, for garnish
    (optional)
Pecorino cheese, grated, for garnish (optional)

To prepare the ragu, heat the oil over medium-high heat in a large pot or Dutch oven. Season the ribs lightly on both sides with salt and pepper. When the oil is sizzling, add the ribs to the pot in a single layer. Brown until golden brown (about 5 minutes) and turn, repeating on the second side. Remove the ribs from the pot and set aside. Drain off all but about 3 tablespoons of fat and turn the heat down to medium. Add the onions and garlic, stirring to coat and to pick up brown bits from the bottom of the pan. Season with salt, pepper, and red pepper flakes and add the bay leaves. Cook until onions are just translucent, about 5 minutes. Add the crushed tomatoes to the pot, bring to a boil, and then reduce to a simmer. Return the ribs to the pot and add the Parmesan rinds. Cook very slowly over low heat for 4 to 6 hours. Remove the ribs, however, as soon as they become very tender but before they are falling apart, after about 3 or 4 hours. (Also remove and discard the bay leaves at this time.) Keep the ribs warm, covered tightly with aluminum foil, in a low oven. Season the sauce to taste and keep warm over low heat.

Next, prepare the duck sausage. Cut the meat away from the bones using a boning knife or paring knife. Discard any sinew or fat. (You can ask your butcher to do the same thing, or buy similarly seasoned prepared duck sausage to save time.) Chop the meat coarsely or grind in a meat grinder set to the smallest size (or ask your butcher to do this). Season the meat with the Italian seasoning. Heat the oil over medium-high heat in a large pot or Dutch oven. Add the seasoned ground duck. Brown gently, stirring occasionally, until evenly browned and cooked through, 8 to 10 minutes. Add the reserved ragu to the pot, stirring well to pick up any brown bits. Bring the ragu to a boil and then reduce to a simmer. Keep warm over low heat.

Meanwhile, prepare the gnudi. To make fresh ricotta (you can substitute approximately ½ cup store-bought ricotta if you prefer), bring the milk up to 200°F in a medium-sized pot over medium-high heat. Add the vinegar and stir. The milk will congeal and form a loose kind of ricotta. Strain the mixture through cheesecloth, pressing out and discarding excess fluid. Refrigerate for 1 hour to set the ricotta.

To make the gnudi, combine the ricotta, flour, egg, and grated Pecorino in a mixer fitted with a pastry paddle on low speed, until the dough has just come together, about 5 minutes. Divide the dough into four small balls, space them on a baking sheet, and let rest in the refrigerator for 30 minutes. To form the gnudi, roll each ball into a log with the palm of your hand on a lightly floured surface. The logs should be about 1 or 2 inches in diameter. Cut each log into 1-inch lengths with a pastry cutter. Set aside on a lightly floured surface. To cook, bring a large pot of well-salted water to a boil. Gently add the gnudi and cook for 3 to 4 minutes, until they float to the surface. Drain well in a colander.

Return the gnudi to the pot and toss with the butter. Season to taste with salt and pepper. Toss lightly with the warm ragu and cubed Scamorza cheese. Serve on individual plates or on a platter, garnishing with fresh basil and a sprinkle of freshly grated Pecorino cheese if desired. Serve 2 or 3 of the warm ribs off to the side of each plate.

LOMBARDI'S ITALIAN RESTAURANT

979 HARBOR VIEW ROAD, JAMES ISLAND
(843) 795-3133
OWNER: VINNY LOMBARDI
CHEF-PROPRIETOR: RICK AGIUS

Red sauce (which Vinny Lombardi calls "gravy") flows like an edible Hudson River at Lombardi's—making it all the better for dipping bread and spooning pasta. By chef Rick Agius's estimation, his kitchen pumps out eight to twelve gallons of the stuff every day. "I was raised on bread dipped in red sauce," says Lombardi, who spent fifty years of his life working as a bath and renovations man before his second wife convinced him to move to Charleston and eventually to open a restaurant. At sixty-eight years old, the New York native jumped into the brave new role of restaurateur and opened Lombardi's because, he "didn't feel like there were any good New York–style Italian restaurants around town."

Though many miles away from the Big Apple, Lombardi's teems with the energy, accents, attitude, and aromas unique to that city. Vinny is always front and center, usually dressed entirely in black and working the front of the house, his strong Brooklyn accent peppered with colorful language and with eye-sparkling charm aplenty.

The recipes are from Vinny's Italian mother's kitchen. Rick, a hard-working hulk, tweaked them with Vinny's blessing. He is in full command of the narrow, open kitchen that emits wave after wave of garlic and delivers towering portions of lasagna, veal, chicken, pasta, and pizza dishes.

This rich, earthy recipe is something Rick has prepared over the years as a chef and at Christmas gatherings with his extended Maltese family. Brian Bertolini of Rio Bertolini's Pasta was generous enough to provide the recipe for the ravioli his company prepares and delivers to Lombardi's. Remember, fresh pasta cooks much more quickly than dried, and ravioli needs to be treated tenderly.

SWEET POTATO RAVIOLI WITH SAGE BROWN BUTTER SAUCE, WALNUTS, AND GORGONZOLA

(Makes approximately 36 to 40 ravioli or 6 servings)

For the pasta:

5 eggs, plus 5 egg yolks
4½ cups semolina or all-purpose flour

For the ravioli filling:

3 large sweet potatoes
3 tablespoons butter
12 fresh sage leaves, finely chopped
1 cup mascarpone

2 tablespoons brown sugar
Dash of allspice
Salt and freshly ground black pepper to taste
1 egg

For the sage brown butter sauce:

2 sticks (½ pound) unsalted butter
16 fresh sage leaves
Salt and freshly ground black pepper to taste
Pinch of nutmeg

For the garnish:

⅔ cup roasted walnuts
¾ cup crumbled Gorgonzola
Freshly ground black pepper to taste (optional)

Begin by preparing the pasta. (It can be prepared a few days ahead and refrigerated, and it also freezes very well.) Combine the eggs, yolks, and flour in a mixer or food processor fitted with a pastry paddle. Blend on low until the dough holds together in a ball. Turn out on a floured surface and knead for 5 minutes, until it's springy and uniform. Let dough rest on the counter, covered loosely with plastic wrap or a slightly damp towel, for 1 hour.

Meanwhile, prepare the filling. Preheat the oven to 425°F. Pierce each sweet potato in several places with a fork or knife. Roast the potatoes until soft throughout, about 45 minutes, depending on their size. Remove from oven and set aside. When cool enough to handle, peel the sweet potatoes and mash until smooth in a large bowl. Brown the butter with the sage in a small sauté pan over medium-high heat. Cook until butter is caramel colored but not burned, about 4 minutes. Combine the browned butter with the remaining ingredients (except the egg) in the bowl with the potatoes. Blend until smooth with a wooden spoon. Taste and adjust salt and pepper as needed.

To roll out and shape the pasta, cut the dough into three equal-sized parts using a chef's knife. On a large lightly floured surface, quickly roll out the pasta either with a rolling pin or a pasta machine to paper thin (you should be able to read a newspaper through it, says Brian). Working quickly, drape the pasta on a pasta dowel or rod as it's rolled out. To make the ravioli, place one layer of pasta on your work surface. Beat the egg with a few drops of water to make an egg wash and brush the pasta with a thin layer. Place a generous tablespoon of the filling on the pasta, arranging spoonfuls in lines spaced about 2-inches apart. Gently drape another layer of pasta on top. Press gently around each mound of filling to seal the pasta (Brian uses PVC pipe to press into and seal the ravioli). Cut into rounds or squares with a crimped pasta cutter. Repeat until all pasta is used. (Cut the third pasta sheet in half to form two equal-sized layers to form the remaining ravioli.) Let the ravioli rest briefly, covered, in the refrigerator.

To prepare the butter, heat a large sauté pan over medium-high heat. Once the butter has melted, add the sage leaves. Continue cooking, allowing the butter to bubble slightly, until the butter has turned a deep golden color. (Do not let the butter burn!) Season to taste with salt and pepper and add the nutmeg. Remove from the heat. (The butter can be prepared up to several days in advance and stored in a sealed container in the refrigerator. Reheat to melt before serving.)

To cook the pasta, bring a large pot of cold, generously salted water to a boil over high heat. Gently place the ravioli in the water, reducing the boil to a rigorous simmer. Cook until al dente, about 2 or 3 minutes (the ravioli will float to the surface when done), and drain well.

To serve, gently toss the hot ravioli with the warm sage butter in the sauté pan. Serve, either on a large platter or on individual plates. Drizzle with the roasted walnuts and crumbled Gorgonzola. If desired, give each plate a final hit of freshly ground black pepper. Serve immediately.

Pane e Vino

17 Warren Street, downtown
(843) 853-5955
www.italydiscovered.com
Owners: Massimiliano ("Massi") and Natasha Sarrocchi
Chef: Marc Jefferson

Pane e Vino (which means "bread and wine" in Italian) is not fancy, but it's warm, authentic, and fabulous. Perhaps Roman-born Massimiliano Sarrocchi says it best: "We don't do fine dining, but we make comfort food that people in Italy eat every day."

"Massi" and his wife, Natasha, take cues from country and regional Italy in the uncluttered menu, with the likes of Sicilian-style fish soup and a simple crostini misti topped with Gorgonzola, black fig spread, and sautéed wild mushrooms. Even the lasagna has a twist—it's made with Fontina cheese and layered with porcini mushrooms and has beef and pork stew for a sauce.

Chef Marc Jefferson and Massi have worked side by side in the restaurant biz since 1995 and still share kitchen duties. "Basically, whatever we randomly feel like making, we go in and make it," says Massi, explaining the daily specials.

This wholly earthy, fragrant dish harks back to Massi's youth in Tuscany, where wild boar hunting was a seasonal and completely communal event. "After the hunt, we would celebrate. Everything gets used; someone makes a ham and another makes a steak. The whole family gets involved, from the old woman making the lasagna to another actually doing the cooking," he explains. In Italy, as in Charleston, this is more of a winter meal, but for different reasons. There, it's because the curing and sausage-making are done in the winter for meats to be consumed through the spring. Here, it's because this dish would be too rich to stomach in August but just begs to be a cold January evening indulgence. The broad, flat noodles cling idyllically to this chunky, flavorful stew.

Wild Boar Stew with Pappardelle
(Serves 6)

2 tablespoons olive oil
1 large onion, diced
3 cloves garlic, crushed
1 carrot, peeled and diced
1–2 tablespoons chopped fresh rosemary
2 pounds wild boar meat (preferably shoulder or leg), tendons and gristle removed, cut into ½-inch cubes

5 whole black peppercorns, crushed, plus more to taste
Salt to taste
4 cups red wine (preferably a full-bodied Italian red)
2 pounds canned peeled and crushed tomatoes
1½ pounds dried pappardelle
½ cup grated pecorino cheese

In a large Dutch oven or stew pot, heat the olive oil over medium-high heat. Add the onion, garlic, carrot, and rosemary. Sauté, stirring, until softened, about 5 minutes. Add the meat to the pan and season with peppercorns and salt. Cook evenly on all sides, turning the cubes as needed, until browned, about 8 minutes. Add wine to just cover the meat and vegetables. Bring to a boil, then reduce to a simmer. Add more wine as needed as the wine reduces. Keep cooking until the meat is literally falling apart; this will take 1 to 2 hours. Then add the crushed tomatoes, bring to a boil, and then reduce to a simmer. Cover partially and cook slowly for 3 hours to achieve a "thick, dark sauce." Season the stew to taste with cracked peppercorns and salt, as needed.

Meanwhile, bring a large pot of generously salted cold water to a boil. Add the pasta all at once and stir to submerge it fully. Cook according to package directions, to al dente, then drain well and return to the pot, over low heat. Pour the stew over the noodles and stir gently but thoroughly to combine. Serve in shallow bowls and sprinkle generously with grated pecorino and cracked pepper.

Bacco

976 Houston Northcutt Boulevard, Mount Pleasant
(843) 884-6969
WWW.BACCOCHARLESTON.COM
Executive Chef/Owner: Michael Scognamiglio

Bad chemistry with a college chemistry class, immediate Italian lineage, a lifetime of good eating, and a passion for Italian cooking eventually aligned the stars to jump-start this young chef's star-worthy culinary career and lead to the opening of this, his first restaurant. Its name the Italian name for the Roman god of food and wine, Bacco is equal parts convivial and delicious.

Set in a small, relatively spartan space off a well-traveled thoroughfare in Mount Pleasant, Bacco attracts loyal locals from all over greater Charleston for its shining Neapolitan and Venetian fare and the infectious joy Michael takes in pleasing and interacting with his clients. "When I look out in the dining room at night, I always see people conversing back and forth from different tables and they don't even know each other. I like that," he says.

Michael personally selects the wine varietals from Sardinia, Campagna, and Piedmont to pair with his "small but round" menu of select dishes, many of which are loose interpretations of those his father prepared while he was growing up, modified to reflect "restaurant style."

This recipe has Venetian undertones and has been on the restaurant's menu since day one. Don't be put off by risotto. The only techniques required to withdraw the starch from Arborio rice are an initial toast, lots of patient stirring, and warm stock. The rest is a snap. "True Venetian-style *risi e bisi* (rice and peas) should be very runny and almost have a soupy consistency," advises Michael. His version is topped with crispy pancetta.

The tasty Parmesan broth provides an excellent opportunity to use up the rinds of past Parmesan cheese rounds you've hopefully been storing in your freezer. (If not, ask the cheese cutter at your grocery for a bunch, or substitute chicken or vegetable broth for a milder, less cheesy flavor.)

Risi e Bisi (Rice and Peas)
(Serves 6)

For the Parmesan broth:

½ gallon water
½ pound Parmesan rinds
1 bay leaf
1½ teaspoons whole black peppercorns
¼ onion

For the risotto:

1 cup diced pancetta (salt-cured Italian bacon, available in most grocery stores)
2 tablespoons olive oil
3 cups Arborio rice (a round, Italian rice with a high starch content)
1 cup fresh or frozen peas
2 tablespoons butter
½ cup freshly grated Parmesan
Salt and freshly ground black pepper to taste

To prepare the broth, combine all of the broth ingredients in a large pot and simmer for 30 to 45 minutes over medium heat, stirring on occasion, to prevent the cheese rinds from sticking to the bottom of the pot. Remove from the heat and strain broth through a fine-mesh strainer. Reserve warm or cool and refrigerate or freeze until you're ready to prepare the risotto. (The broth should keep, refrigerated in an airtight container, for up to a week and in the freezer for several months.)

To prepare the risotto, heat a medium sauté pan over medium-high heat and add the pancetta. Cook, tossing occasionally, until the pancetta is golden brown and crispy, about 5 minutes. Remove from the pan and drain on paper towels. Meanwhile, heat the olive oil in a medium pot over medium-high heat. Add the rice and sauté (toasting the rice) for 30 seconds, stirring constantly. (This "wakes up" the rice and prepares it for the all-important broth absorption process.) Add about 2½ cups of the warm Parmesan broth, or enough to just cover the rice, and cook over medium heat for 15 minutes, stirring constantly. Add additional broth in ¼-cup increments, if needed to keep the rice moist. Add the peas and continue cooking for another 2 to 3 minutes, stirring constantly and adding small amounts of broth if the rice appears to be getting dry.

The risotto will need 20 to 25 minutes to cook to al dente. When done, remove from the heat and stir in the butter and grated Parmesan. Season to taste with salt and pepper. Serve in shallow bowls and sprinkle each bowl with pancetta. Serve immediately. Risotto waits for no one!

Il Cortile del Re

193A King Street, downtown
(843) 853-1888
Owners: Kim Green and Alfredo Temelini

A vintage black-and-white photograph of an American woman in Italy hangs near the long wooden bar at this intimate *enoteca* (wine bar) and trattoria situated on the antique store–lined quiet end of King Street. "It follows me wherever I go," says co-owner Kim Green of the photo.

That's entirely fitting, because a love of Italy led the Delaware, Maryland, native to Italy, where she lived for many years before she fell in love with Charleston and moved here with the intention of opening a small *enoteca*. Her love of Italy still lives in her heart and at Il Cortile del Re (Italian for "courtyard of the king"). The restaurant was so popular from its opening day thirteen years ago, it almost spontaneously morphed into the more extensive full-blown trattoria it is today.

Co-owner Alfredo Temelini hails from Italy and works with Kim to bring the flavors of Tuscany to each and every plate. The following is a recipe that Alfredo's grandmother regularly prepared for him. "If you grow up in Italy, you know how to cook, especially if you learned how to cook from your grandmother," says Kim. This recipe is simple and delicious. The chunky, creamy sauce practically begs for penne, but Kim says it's fine to serve it with your pasta of choice.

Penne al Tre Sapori

(Serves 4 to 6)

3 tablespoons extra-virgin olive oil
1 cup julienned asparagus, cut into 2-inch strips
½ cup julienned pancetta, cut into 2-inch strips
1 cup sliced cremini mushrooms
1 tablespoon finely chopped garlic
1 tablespoon finely chopped fresh rosemary,
   plus a few sprigs for garnish (optional)
1 cup diced onion
2 tablespoons salt
1 tablespoon freshly ground black pepper
1 quart heavy whipping cream
1 cup milk
1 pound dried penne (or another pasta)
¼ cup grated pecorino cheese

To prepare the sauce, heat the olive oil over high heat in a large saucepan. Add the asparagus, pancetta, mushrooms, garlic, rosemary, onion, salt, and pepper and sauté, occasionally stirring, over high heat until just wilted, about 3 minutes. Add the cream and milk and stir. Bring up to a low boil, then reduce to a simmer over medium-low heat. Simmer sauce gently for 30 to 45 minutes.

As the sauce approaches completion, bring a large pot of generously salted water to a boil over high heat. Add the pasta, stir, and cook according to the package directions. Remove from the heat and drain well. Return the pasta to the pot and dress with the sauce, tossing well to coat. Serve in individual shallow bowls or on a large serving platter, sprinkled with grated pecorino cheese. Garnish with a few sprigs of fresh rosemary if desired. *Buon appetito!*

Seafood

An eternally proud bunch, Charlestonians are fond of referring to the brackish waters that form the port and envelop the peninsula and islands as the place "where the Ashley and Cooper Rivers meet to form the Atlantic." That may be disputable, but what is not is the fact that Charleston is literally surrounded by water—rivers, an ocean, marshes, tributaries—and in those waters resides a rich population of fish and crustaceans unique to the climate and geography of the area. Triggerfish, wreckfish, red drum, and other fish, along with the Lowcountry's famous bounty of briny shrimp and oysters, fall temptingly into the talented hands of the chefs in this chapter, who demand local fresh fish in their kitchens. Simplicity was the across-the-board battle cry in talking with these chefs about working with fish, but boring was most decidedly not.

Take Blossom's Adam Close's version of fried shrimp, a decadent flutter of buttermilk-soaked lightly battered shrimp nestled on a bed of sweet creamed corn laced with salty strips of prosciutto. He tops it off with a tart, spicy tomato marmalade. At Bowen's Island Restaurant, Robert Barber's Frogmore Stew comes straight from the heart of the Lowcountry, while Hank's Frank McMahon pairs a blue cheese vinaigrette, chunky with sweet corn and green tomatoes, with pan-sautéed wreckfish.

Fish dishes from Italian restaurants Fulton Five and Mercato use Sicilian and North African ingredients like cinnamon and cloves to create Venetian Marinated Snapper and Local Shrimp and Fregula Stew, while Anson's Kevin Johnson and Old Village Post House's Jim Walker share two ways to make an old Lowcountry favorite, shrimp and grits.

Blossom

171 East Bay Street, downtown
(843) 722-9200
www.magnolia-blossom-cypress.com
Executive Chef: Adam Close

Sandwiched between her taller sister restaurants, Magnolias and Cypress, on a restaurant-rich stretch on bustling East Bay, Blossom has experienced occasional bouts of shaky culinary identity. Initially an Italian restaurant when it opened more than fifteen years ago, the restaurant still retains a smattering of luscious fresh pastas and smoky gourmet pizzas served fresh from the dazzling mosaic-tile wood fireplace. Executive chef Adam Close, at the helm here since 2006, has nurtured this always beautiful slow bloomer into a showstopper of a seafood restaurant.

A devotee of simplicity and precision, the Johnson & Wales grad would never dream of muddling the sweetness of Lowcountry shrimp (which he correctly describes as the "best in the world") or mixing the milky purity of local flounder with conflicting complicated ingredients. Instead, exclusively local fish and local seasonal produce meet in memorable dishes like crab cakes kissed with the freshness of tarragon (an idea he got from mentor Donald Barickman, when he worked at Magnolias) and in the dashing flavor plays in this fried shrimp recipe.

What Adam loves about this combination is that the hot (and he insists they have to be hot and fresh out of the fryer) shrimp sits upon the creamed corn, so it doesn't get soggy. A gorgeous, synergistic dish that is not complicated to make, this will become a favorite in any shrimp lover's kitchen. When you visit Charleston, try to purchase some of her celebrated shrimp, freezing them in a milk carton filled with water and bringing them home with you to prepare this dish. Then you will see what all the fuss is about!

Buttermilk Fried Shrimp with Creamed Corn, Shaved Prosciutto, and Spicy Tomato Marmalade
(Serves 4)

For the tomato marmalade:

2 tablespoons extra-virgin olive oil
2 tablespoons finely diced shallot
1 teaspoon minced garlic
2 cups red wine vinegar
¾ cup granulated sugar
4 medium tomatoes, seeded and chopped
　　into medium dice

For the corn:

2 cups heavy cream
½ cup grated Parmesan cheese
3 cups fresh corn kernels (cut from about 4 ears)
2 tablespoons very thin strips prosciutto
Salt and freshly ground black pepper to taste

For the shrimp:

1 pound large (21–25 count) South Carolina
 shrimp (substitute shrimp from another
 region if you must)
2 quarts vegetable oil
4 cups all-purpose flour
2 tablespoons kosher salt
1 tablespoon garlic powder
2 tablespoons freshly ground black pepper
1 cup buttermilk
1 egg

To prepare the marmalade, heat the oil over medium heat in a medium saucepan. Add the shallot and garlic. Sweat over low heat until the shallot is translucent, but not brown, about 3 minutes. Add the vinegar and sugar, bring to a boil, and cook until reduced by half. Remove from the heat and stir in the tomatoes. Place in the refrigerator to cool. Once cool, puree slightly with a handheld blender or a food processor to

a medium-chunky consistency. Set aside. (The marmalade can be made 2 to 3 days in advance and refrigerated in a covered container. It can be reheated and served warm or served at room temperature.)

Next, prepare the creamed corn. In a medium saucepan, bring the heavy cream to a simmer over medium heat. Continue cooking until it's reduced by half. Add the Parmesan, corn, and prosciutto. Continue to cook and reduce for an additional 5 minutes or until the mixture is thick and creamy. Season to taste with salt and pepper. Keep warm over very low heat or a water bath until ready to serve. (The corn can be prepared ahead, refrigerated, and reheated before serving. However, it is best freshly prepared, to get a real snap out of the corn.)

To prepare the shrimp, peel and devein the shrimp (see sidebar, page 49), leaving the tails intact for presentation. Bring the oil up to 350°F in a large pot over medium-high heat or an electric fryer. Meanwhile, combine the flour, salt, garlic powder, and pepper in a shallow mixing bowl and set aside. Combine the buttermilk and egg in another bowl, beating slightly with a fork to make an egg wash. In batches, dredge the shrimp in the flour mixture and coat completely, tapping off any excess flour. Next, dip each floured shrimp in the egg wash and then again in the flour mixture. The shrimp should be completely coated with flour and feel dry to the touch.

To cook, carefully place half of the shrimp in the hot oil and cook for 3 minutes. Remove shrimp from the oil with a slotted spoon and place on a paper towel–lined plate to drain. Repeat the cooking process with the remaining shrimp.

To plate, place equal quantities of the creamed corn on four attractive plates and arrange the shrimp in a decorative pattern over the corn. Offer the marmalade in a ramekin or off to the side for a snappy dipping sauce. Serve immediately.

Bowen's Island Restaurant

1871 Bowen's Island Road, Folly Island
(843) 795-2757
www.bowensislandrestaurant.com
Owner: Robert Barber

Equally legendary for its succulent steamed oysters and never-ending graffiti stockpile, Bowen's is literally a tumbledown shack of a place. It's surrounded by piles of white half-forgotten oyster shells and drenched with palpable memories of easy times spent at the water's edge drinking beer and slurping down oysters with good friends.

Before it was a restaurant, Bowen's was a fish camp where Robert's grandparents cooked fish and shrimp in a skillet and roasted oysters over an open fire for their overnight camp guests. Robert took over the business upon his grandmother's death two decades ago. By that time, the restaurant had morphed into a Lowcountry must-do-before-you-die legend. Indeed, Robert was honored with a James Beard Award in 2006, which deemed Bowen's an American classic.

The simple menu here features mostly boiled and fried local seafood along with another Lowcountry classic, Frogmore Stew. Also called "Lowcountry Boil" and "Beaufort Stew," it originally got its name from a section of St. Helena Island near Beaufort (about an hour and a half south of Charleston) where the dish was created. For Bowen's version, Robert insists upon Hillshire Farm smoked kielbasa ("It's got more bite and texture," he says) and not overcooking the shrimp. "You can cook all of 'em (corn, potatoes, sausage) too long, but if you overcook the shrimp, it's messed up," he says. He's right. Stir the shrimp in at the very end and let the heat from the broth cook them just right before serving. This is a comforting meal that cooks in a single pot in minutes.

Bowen's Island Frogmore Stew
(Serves 6)

6–8 cups cold water
3 tablespoons Old Bay Seasoning
Dash of Texas Pete Hot Sauce (or your preferred brand)
1 stick (¼ pound) unsalted butter (optional)
1½ pounds new red potatoes
1½–2 pounds Hillshire Farm smoked kielbasa, cut into 1- to 2-inch lengths
6 ears corn, shucked and broken in half
2 pounds shell-on fresh shrimp, 20-24 count

Place the cold water, Old Bay Seasoning, hot sauce, and butter, if using, in a large pot. (The amount of water depends on the size of your pot. You should have enough space to let the ingredients breathe and move and enough water to barely cover them.) Bring the seasoned water to a boil over high heat. Once boiling, add the potatoes and cook for 10 to 15 minutes or until the potatoes are soft when pierced with a fork. Reduce the heat to medium-high. Add the kielbasa and corn and cook for another 5 minutes. Increase the heat to high and bring the mixture back to a boil. (It must be at a boil before adding the shrimp.) Add the shrimp all at once and remove pot from the heat. Stir gently to mix in the shrimp and keep watching until the shrimp start to turn pink. Drain the stew in a large colander and return to the pot. Serve immediately on a large

platter or on individual plates; Robert uses a rustic copper or wooden bowl to serve at the restaurant. Across the Lowcountry, this dish is often served on tables covered with newspaper. Try it at home for an especially authentic feeling.

HANK'S

10 HAYNE STREET, DOWNTOWN
(843) 723-3474
WWW.HANKSSEAFOODRESTAURANT.COM
EXECUTIVE CHEF: FRANK MCMAHON

A serendipitous combination of Frank McMahon's desire to move from the West Coast to the East Coast and a phone call to his wife from a Charleston-based headhunter brought the couple to Charleston in 1994. They haven't left since. A Culinary Institute of America grad with a fat, impressive résumé, including posts at New York's Le Bernadin and Santa Monica's Opus, McMahon was heading up another prestigious establishment and Relais Chateaux property here (McCrady's, see page 148), when local entrepreneur extraordinaire Hank Holliday approached him and told him he wanted to re-create a "really good" seafood restaurant in downtown's historic district. "And that was all she wrote," says the good-humored Frank in his musical Irish accent.

Hank was inspired by his memories of a long-defunct Charleston restaurant classic, Henry's, which was of the white tablecloth seafood variety. While he envisioned fried seafood at Hank's, Frank initially balked and insisted the restaurant would have to be at least partially "contemporary." The two met in the middle to create Hank's special blend of Southern and Lowcountry contemporary cuisine, in a manly setting awash in dark, gleaming woods, leather, and yes, white linen tablecloths. An expansive raw bar and a practically life-size mural of Hank decked out in a white apron, holding a massive lobster, dominate, contributing to the old-world men's club feel of the place.

Frank's mantra is simplicity, and he loves embellishing fish and seafood with vinaigrettes, as in this recipe, which showcases Charleston's very own wreckfish (see sidebar, page 131), a meaty, moist fish remotely related to grouper and snapper (which can be substituted when wreckfish is unavailable) in flavor and texture.

WRECKFISH WITH GREEN TOMATO, SWEET CORN, AND BLUE CHEESE VINAIGRETTE
(Serves 4)

For the vinaigrette:

1 cup cored, chopped green tomatoes
1 medium ear sweet corn, shucked
¼ cup chopped scallions
2 tablespoons chopped chives
Salt and freshly ground black pepper to taste
1 cup double-strength chicken stock (prepare by reducing 2 cups of unsalted chicken stock)
¼ cup champagne vinegar or apple cider vinegar
½ cup extra-virgin olive oil
¼ cup crumbled blue cheese

For the fish:

4 6-ounce wreckfish fillets
Salt and freshly ground black pepper to taste
2 tablespoons olive oil
2 tablespoons butter

Preheat the oven to 350°F. To prepare the vinaigrette, core the tomatoes and cut into medium dice. Roast the corn on the cob in the oven for 20 minutes, or until golden brown. Allow to cool. Cut the corn from the cob and place in a medium bowl with the diced tomato. Add the scallions and chives and season with salt and pepper. Cover this mixture with the chicken stock and vinegar. Mix gently, then whisk in the olive oil and blue cheese. Add salt and pepper to taste.

Season the fish on both sides with salt and pepper. Heat a large skillet over medium-high heat and add the olive oil and butter. When sizzling, add the wreckfish filets in a single, well-spaced layer. Cook for 4 to 6 minutes (depending on the thickness of the fillets), turn, and repeat. Serve immediately on individual plates, topped with a generous serving of the vinaigrette.

THE CHARLESTON BUMP

The Charleston Bump, where wreckfish thrive, rises off the surrounding Blake Plateau, which is located roughly 100 miles offshore from South Carolina and Georgia. Depths here range from an astonishing 1,300 to 3,000 feet of tumultuous water, swirling with eddies and rapid, mean currents. It makes for an unusual combination of tough fishing and a happy habitat for wreckfish, which embrace its spooky universe of deep-water corals and caves. It's also the exclusive spawning and United States–based hunting ground for wreckfish, a wholly sustainable fish that is monitored by the state and federal governments. The fish is named for its fondness for lurking in and around wreckage and debris.

FULTON FIVE

5 FULTON STREET, DOWNTOWN
(843) 853-555
WWW.FULTONFIVE.NET
EXECUTIVE CHEF: BRIAN PARKHURST

This northern Italian cuisine retreat has long been considered Charleston's most romantic dining destination. It certainly is that, all wrapped up in tiny sparkling white lights, cushioned by warming pale green walls, and set off a tiny lane of a one-way street downtown. Though she's only a few years shy of celebrating her twentieth birthday, Fulton Five still retains a fresh, youthful luster.

Much of that credit has to go to chef Brian Parkhurst, a would-be cop who eventually succumbed to the allure of cooking for a living. For Brian, simplicity and top-quality fresh ingredients are absolutely mandatory. He is also a self-professed cookbook addict: "I get my hands on every Italian cookbook I can, read it, and then put a new twist on the dishes that intrigue me," he explains. His interpretation of Bolognese sauce, for example, includes finely chopped chicken livers and the kick of "medieval spices" like cinnamon, cloves, and nutmeg. Similarly, this recipe, an interpretation of a Venetian-style dish he learned from local chef and good friend, Jacques Larson, deliciously escorts both sweet and savory flavors to an elegant bow with the blush of both cinnamon and cloves. It can be prepared up to 48 hours in advance and should be served at room temperature, rendering it a perfect dish for non-harried entertaining.

VENETIAN MARINATED SNAPPER

(Makes 4 small portions or 2 entrée portions)

1½ cups extra-virgin olive oil

2 pounds fresh red snapper fillets (or substitute another mild fish, such as yellowtail) for four ½-pound fillets

Salt and freshly ground black pepper to taste

¾ cup all-purpose flour

1 large yellow onion, thinly sliced

1¼ cups red wine vinegar

8 cloves

1 cinnamon stick

¼ cup golden raisins

¾ cup granulated sugar

¼ cup pine nuts

4 cups baby mixed lettuce

Heat 1 cup of olive oil in a large sauté pan over medium-high heat until hot and almost smoking. Meanwhile, season the fish well on both sides with salt and pepper. Place the flour on a shallow plate and dredge each fillet in the flour, tapping off any excess. Arrange the fish evenly in the pan in a single layer (be careful not to overcrowd). Fry for about 4 minutes, or until golden brown, carefully turn, and fry on the other side. Remove the fish from the pan and drain on paper towels.

Heat ¼ cup of olive oil in a medium sauté pan over medium heat. Add the onion and cook, stirring occasionally, until softened and golden brown, 10 to 12 minutes. Pour the vinegar over the onions in the pan. Tie the cloves and cinnamon stick together in a little cheesecloth pouch and add the pouch, the golden raisins, and the sugar to the onion mixture. Increase the heat to high and boil for 8 to 10 minutes, reducing the vinegar down to a sauce. Remove pan from the heat.

Arrange the fish fillets in a shallow, nonreactive baking dish in a single layer. Remove the spice pouch from the onion mixture and pour the warm blend evenly over the fish. Cover tightly and refrigerate for 24 to 48 hours.

Remove the marinated fish from the refrigerator several hours before serving to allow it to come to room temperature. Just before serving, toast the pine nuts over high heat in a small sauté pan, shaking from time to time, until warm and golden brown. Toss the greens with the remaining ¼ cup of olive oil and salt and pepper in a small bowl. Place a mound of the dressed lettuce on each plate and top with a fish fillet and a portion of the marinade. Scatter the warm toasted pine nuts over the top.

MUSE

82 SOCIETY STREET, DOWNTOWN
(834) 577-1102
WWW.CHARLESTONMUSE.COM
EXECUTIVE CHEF: JASON HOUSER

This eclectic Mediterranean gem looks to Pompeii and the Villa of the Mysteries' famous frescoes, along with the myriad cuisines and ingredients of the Mediterranean, as its multifarious muse. Murals of the muses of Spain, Italy, France, and Greece adorn this rambling circa-1850 dollhouse like so many rays of merry light on a sparkling sea. Situated on a quiet, residential street in the heart of downtown, Muse embodies intimacy and whimsy in one colorful fell swoop.

Executive chef Jason Houser abandoned his study of Tibetan Buddhism at the College of Charleston to pursue what would become his true calling—cooking—which he describes as "meditative." He's traveled through France, Spain, Italy, and Greece and worked along with some of Charleston's best to arrive at the enlightened culinary place he revels in today.

At Muse, his goal is to take ingredients from various Mediterranean countries and "jumble them all up"—thoughtfully. This recipe gets inspiration from Southerners' penchant for fried seafood, but Jason prefers to keep the fish whole (bones removed), the way that Mediterranean sea bass ("bronzini") is commonly served in Europe. It's a compelling presentation and just fabulous with the acidic edge of orange and smoothness of pureed cauliflower. If you can't find bronzini, substitute red snapper, which has a similar mild flavor and creamy texture. Because removing the bones while leaving the head and tail intact is a challenging notion for most home cooks, just leave the bones in and ask your fishmonger to gut the fish for you and, if possible, remove the spine and ribs. Alternatively, you could just fry fillets following the directions below.

LIGHTLY FRIED WHOLE MEDITERRANEAN SEA BASS OVER CAULIFLOWER PUREE WITH AN ORANGE SAFFRON BUTTER SAUCE AND FRIED BASIL
(Serves 4)

For the cauliflower puree:

1 head cauliflower
¼ cup canola oil
Salt and freshly ground black pepper

For the butter sauce:

2 cups fresh-squeezed orange juice
   (do not use concentrate)
1 cup white wine
1 shallot, thinly sliced
10 fennel seeds, toasted briefly to release flavor
½ teaspoon saffron
5 whole black peppercorns
1 bay leaf
Salt and freshly ground black pepper to taste
2 sticks (½ pound) cold butter, cut into
   16 tablespoon-sized pieces

For the fish and garnish:

8 cups canola oil
16 fresh basil leaves
4 small whole bronzini (Mediterranean sea bass),
    gutted
Salt and freshly ground black pepper to taste
2 cups semolina

To prepare the cauliflower puree, cut the cauliflower into quarters and remove any tough stems from the center of each quarter's core. Break off the florets using your fingers. Heat canola oil in a large sauté pan over medium heat and add the cauliflower. Season with salt and pepper once the cauliflower hits the pan, and cook until tender, stirring occasionally, 10 to 12 minutes. Be careful not to brown the cauliflower. When cauliflower is tender, transfer to a food processor and puree until smooth and light. Keep puree warm over a gently simmering water bath.

To prepare the butter sauce, combine the orange juice, white wine, shallot, fennel seed, saffron, peppercorns, and bay leaf in a medium saucepan and bring to a boil over high heat. Reduce the heat to medium-high and continue to cook until the sauce is reduced by two-thirds. Season with salt and pepper. Reduce the heat to medium. To finish, gradually incorporate the cold butter, 2 tablespoons at a time, by whisking the butter into the warm sauce to form an emulsion. The sauce should not ever boil, and it should become cohesive and frothy with a brilliant orange color. Continue adding butter until it is all incorporated. Strain the sauce through a fine-mesh sieve and keep warm over a gently simmering water bath.

To cook the garnish and fish, heat 8 cups of canola oil in a large pot over medium-high heat to 400°F. When the oil has reached that temperature, throw the basil leaves in all at once and fry for 15 seconds. They will sizzle and pop

and turn a brilliant green. Remove the leaves with a slotted spoon and drain on paper towels.

Season the fish on both sides. Place the flour in a shallow bowl and dredge the fish in the flour, tapping off any excess. Fry the fish, one at a time, until cooked through and golden brown (2 to 3 minutes for a 1½-pound bronzini, less for fillets).

To serve, evenly distribute the warm cauliflower puree among four plates. Place the fish on top of the puree, "as if it were swimming," says Jason. Spoon several tablespoons of the warm sauce around the edges of the plate and garnish with 4 fried basil leaves.

MERCATO

102 NORTH MARKET STREET, DOWNTOWN
(843) 722-6393
WWW.MERCATOCHARLESTON.COM
EXECUTIVE CHEF: EDDIE MORAN

During busy months of the year, guests at this sleek, cosmopolitan Northern Italian–style eatery have to negotiate the bump and grind of tourists near the entrance, which happens to flank the northern side of the popular Old City Market. It's a small price to pay. Inside awaits a deep red and tan marble oasis of urban tranquility and some of the best food the city has to offer, crafted by executive chef Eddie Moran.

The San Francisco native is a recent transplant to Charleston and Mercato, but he espouses old-fashioned classic technique in his kitchen. "First and foremost, I'm a cook, and I like to cook like they cook in Italy, using seasonal ingredients at all times," says Eddie.

Simple, maybe, but amazingly subtle and layered, Eddie's interpretations of the likes of Veal Cheek Ravioli with Wild Mushroom Sugo and soothing Baked Gnocco of Semolina and Parmesan and Fontina Cheeses with Fried Rosemary testify to his spot-on culinary instincts and his use of best-quality ingredients. This dynamic dish borrows from North Africa's cupboard. Fregula, a Sardinian semolina wheat pasta that recalls Israeli couscous, wraps around a heady tomato sauce spiked with enticing notes of sweet and savory, balanced by the buttery qualities of always local shrimp. Best of all, it comes together in minutes.

LOCAL SHRIMP AND FREGULA STEW
(Serves 4)

Salt
½ pound fregula (Sardinian couscous)
¼ cup extra-virgin olive oil, plus extra for drizzling
1 white onion, finely chopped
½ cup thinly sliced leeks
2 cloves garlic, minced
Leaves from 4 sprigs fresh oregano, finely chopped
6 anchovy fillets or 2 tablespoons anchovy paste
½ cup chopped flat-leaf parsley
1 teaspoon harissa or 2 teaspoons red pepper flakes
1–1½ pounds extra-large (16–20 count) shrimp, peeled and deveined
1 cup white wine
2¾ cups high-quality prepared marinara sauce
¼ cup currants
¼ cup toasted pine nuts
¼ cup sliced caper berries

Freshly ground black pepper to taste
Sturdy country-style Italian or French bread boule or baguette

Bring a large pot of water with 1 teaspoon salt to a boil over high heat. Add the fregula and cook 7 to 9 minutes, or until al dente. Drain well, reserving 2 cups of the pasta cooking water for the stew. Set aside.

Meanwhile, in a large heavy nonreactive pot, heat the olive oil over medium-high heat. Add the onion, leeks, and garlic and cook, stirring until softened, about 5 minutes. Add the oregano, anchovies, parsley, and harissa and stir, mashing the anchovies with the tines of a fork. Add shrimp and cook until they just begin turning pink, about 3 minutes. Add the wine and cook down until it has reduced by one-third. Mix the prepared marinara sauce with the reserved pasta water and add to the pot. Increase the heat to high and bring the mixture to a boil. Add the cooked fregula, currants, pine nuts, and caper berries. Season to taste with

kosher salt and pepper. Stir well to combine and ladle the stew into individual soup tureens or large shallow bowls. Drizzle each lightly with olive oil. Serve with warm bread or enjoy it as is.

THE RED DRUM

803 COLEMAN BOULEVARD, MOUNT PLEASANT
(843) 849-0313
WWW.REDDRUMRESTAURANT.COM
CHEF-OWNER: BEN BERRYHILL

"South by Southwest" is how Ben Berryhill describes both himself and the food he prepares at Red Drum, a warm, winning Southwestern standout. The Houston native spent summers on his grandparents' east Texas working farm, cooking huge spreads of ham, beans, biscuits, and cornbread for the farmhands with his "country cook" grandmother, and winters working through recipes with his "cookbook chef" mom.

Ben's professional career began with cooking at pizza joints in Hawaii, but it reached its pre–Red Drum pinnacle while Ben was working with Robert Del Grande at Café Annie in Houston. It was there that the Culinary Institute of America grad drank in the subtle, analytic culinary approach of Del Grande, whom Ben calls "a founding father of Southwestern cooking."

Ben is without question Charleston's founding father of Southwestern cuisine. Prior to his restaurant's opening in 2005, there was a total dearth of the piquant stuff here. Red Drum—a name for a local fish—brings it on big time, in dishes like wood-grilled barbecue-bathed Lowcountry shrimp paired with sweet corn pudding and a green chile butter sauce. The mood is always convivial here. The bar bounces with what Ben calls "local *Cheers* feel," while the spacious dining room is soothed by the snap-crackle-pop of real wood fires, hulking beams brought in from a farm in North Carolina, and locally crafted ironwork.

This salmon dish is representative of Ben's mission to use indigenous ingredients stamped with signature Southwestern style. He shared this—the recipe for the most popular dish at Red Drum—exclusively for this book. The corn pudding is probably one of the best things you'll ever put in your mouth.

WOOD-GRILLED SALMON WITH RED PEPPER PUREE AND SWEET CORN PUDDING
(Serves 6)

For the red pepper puree:

4 red bell peppers
2 tablespoons olive oil
1 carrot, peeled and coarsely chopped
1 small onion, coarsely chopped
4 cloves garlic, coarsely chopped
2 red jalapeños, seeded and chopped
Salt and freshly ground black pepper to taste
¼ cup white wine
2 cups chicken stock
⅛ cup heavy cream

For the corn pudding:

24 ears fresh corn, shucked
1 stick (¼ pound) cold unsalted butter,
    cut into 8 tablespoon-sized pieces
2 shallots, finely minced
¾ cup heavy cream
Salt and freshly ground black pepper to taste

For the salmon:

1 pound hickory or oak wood chips
6 6-ounce salmon fillets, skin removed
Salt and freshly ground black pepper to taste
½ cup melted butter

To prepare the red pepper puree, begin by roasting the red bell peppers (see page 95). In a medium pot, heat the olive oil over medium heat. Add the carrot, onion, garlic, and jalapeños, season lightly with salt and pepper, and stir until the vegetables have softened, about 5 minutes. Deglaze the pot with the white wine and cook over medium-high heat until the wine is reduced by half, about 1 minute. Add the chicken stock and simmer over low heat for 25 minutes. Add the heavy cream and roasted red peppers and simmer for 10 more minutes. Remove pot from the stove and cool. Puree in a blender or food processor until smooth. Return puree to a medium saucepan, taste, and adjust salt and pepper as needed. Add cream to finish. Set puree aside. (Note: The puree can be made 2 to 3 days in advance, but don't add the cream until just before serving.)

To prepare the corn pudding, preheat the oven to 350°F. Grate the corn with a large box grater, using the medium or large holes, into a 2-quart, ovenproof casserole dish. (This process helps extract the essential juices from the corn. The cobs should be dry, but do not cut too deeply into the hard part of the cob.) This will yield about 6 cups of grated corn. Cover the casserole tightly with foil and bake for 25 minutes. Remove foil, stir to move any corn that is dry or starting to brown away from the edges, and cook uncovered for an additional 10 to 15 minutes. Remove the casserole from the oven and cool slightly. The corn should look like a semi-dry corn paste.

Heat a large sauté pan over medium to medium-high heat. Add 2 tablespoons of the butter and the minced shallots, stirring. Cook, sweating the shallots until translucent, about 5 minutes. Add the heavy cream and increase the heat to high, bringing the mixture to a boil. Add the corn and season to taste with salt and pepper. When the corn starts to bubble, remove from the heat and gradually stir in the remaining butter, until just melted. Keep warm over a double boiler or gentle water bath until ready to serve.

To prepare the salmon, soak the wood chips for about 2 hours before grilling. Heat a gas or charcoal grill to medium hot. Drain the soaked chips and scatter over the hot coals, or place the damp wood chips on a roasting sheet off to the side of the grill if you're cooking over gas. Season the salmon with salt and freshly ground black pepper. Brush the fillets with the melted butter on both sides to prevent sticking. Place the salmon on the grill and cover. Cook for about 3 minutes (depending on thickness and desired doneness) on the first side and turn, repeating on the second side, keeping the grill covered.

To serve, reheat the red pepper puree. Place a pool of the corn pudding in the center of each plate. Top with a fillet of salmon. Spoon some of the puree all around the center of the plate.

HOW SWEET IT IS

If you sup at Red Drum, don't miss pastry chef Lauren Mitterer's simply sweet dessert concoctions. Nominated for Best Pastry Chef of the Southeast by the James Beard Foundation in 2008, the up-and-coming star knocks socks off with satin-smooth Lemon Flan and Southern Fried Peaches with Bourbon-Blueberry Compote.

ANSON RESTAURANT

12 ANSON STREET, DOWNTOWN
(843) 577-0551
WWW.ANSONRESTAURANT.COM
EXECUTIVE CHEF: KEVIN JOHNSON

Pretty in pink, wrought iron, and delicate French doors, Anson recalls the look and feel of New Orleans's French Quarter, but she is 100 percent Lowcountry. The old gal's been around for nearly twenty years, but in executive chef Kevin Johnson's hands, her cuisine tastes as fresh as ever. He refuses to restrict his larder to cliché Lowcountry ingredients like she-crab and okra, while embracing a broad range of locally raised produce for inspiration. "If one of our farmers is growing it, it's basically in the box. Braised radishes may not necessarily be considered Lowcountry, but if our farmers are growing it, we'll use it. This has really allowed us to think on a different level for inspiration," says Kevin.

To wit, the former vegetarian brings in a whole pig every week and breaks it down into chops and tenderloins, crafting liver terrines, pork belly, and more. Bacon is cured in-house and shrimp stock is prepared from local shrimp. Whole dried corn grown in South Carolina is delivered and ground in the restaurant's very own stone gristmill, which separates the ground corn into grits, cornmeal, and polenta. These are used handily in dishes like cornmeal-dusted okra, cornmeal-fried okra, and, of course, Johnson's memorable take on shrimp and grits, which marries the round mouthfeel of braised pork belly with sweet local shrimp. (Ask your butcher a few days in advance to cut and reserve the pork belly.)

ANSON'S GRITS WITH SHRIMP AND BRAISED BACON
(Serves 6)

For the braised bacon:

1 teaspoon fennel seed
1 teaspoon coriander seed
1 teaspoon cumin seed
Pinch of red pepper flakes
½ teaspoon whole black peppercorns
1 whole star anise
⅛ teaspoon cloves
⅛ teaspoon whole allspice
1 tablespoon salt
1 tablespoon brown sugar
2 pounds fresh pork belly
1 tablespoon olive oil
½ onion
½ carrot, peeled
1 stalk celery
Sodium-free chicken stock or water to cover
2–3 sprigs fresh thyme
1–2 bay leaves

For the grits:

6 cups water
2 cups stone-ground grits
1 cup heavy cream
3 tablespoons unsalted butter
Salt and freshly ground black pepper to taste

For the shrimp stock:

1 tablespoon vegetable oil
1 quart raw shrimp shells
½ cup finely diced onion
1 small carrot, peeled and finely diced
1 stalk celery, finely diced
1 teaspoon fennel seed
4 whole black peppercorns
1 bay leaf
3 sprigs fresh thyme
5 parsley stems
2 tablespoons tomato paste
¼ cup dry white wine

For the sauce and to finish:

2 pounds vine-ripe tomatoes
1½–2 pounds large (21–25 count) shrimp,
    peeled and deveined
Salt and freshly ground black pepper to taste
2 tablespoons butter
6–8 scallions, thinly sliced

Up to 3 days ahead, prepare the spice rub and
marinate the pork belly. Place the fennel seed,
coriander seed, cumin seed, red pepper flakes,
peppercorns, whole star anise, cloves, and
whole allspice in a medium skillet preheated
over medium-high heat. Toast, tossing, until the
spices release their aromas and take on a light
color, about 2 minutes. Remove from the pan and
grind in a spice grinder or small food processor.
Transfer spices to a small bowl and combine with
the salt and the brown sugar. Rub the mixture
evenly into all sides of the pork belly. Place the
belly in an ovenproof casserole dish and cover
tightly with plastic wrap. Refrigerate overnight or
for up to 2 days.

Preheat the oven to 300°F 4 to 5 hours before you plan to serve this dish. Heat the olive oil in a small pot over medium heat. Add the onion, carrot, and celery and sauté for about 3 minutes. Add just enough stock or water to cover the vegetables. Add the thyme and bay leaves. Remove the pork belly from the refrigerator and remove the plastic wrap. Pour the vegetables, stock, and herbs over the belly to just cover it. Cover the casserole dish tightly with aluminum foil. Bake for 4 to 5 hours, or until the pork is easily pierced with a fork. Remove the pork from the liquid and cool. Cut the belly into 1-ounce cubes and set aside, discarding the cooking liquid.

About 2 hours before serving, prepare the grits. Bring the water to a boil in a medium saucepan. Add the grits and whisk thoroughly to combine. Reduce the heat to low and cook for 1 hour or until the grits are tender, stirring very frequently with a flat-tipped wooden spatula. You may need to add a little extra water if they seem too thick. Once the grits are tender and the water is absorbed, add the cream and butter and stir to combine. Season to taste with salt and pepper. Keep the grits warm over low heat or a water bath for up to 2 hours, adding more cream if needed.

Meanwhile, prepare the shrimp stock. In a medium pot, heat the vegetable oil over high heat. When very hot, add the shrimp shells. (Use the shells from the shrimp for the sauce or ask your fishmonger for some. Whenever you have shrimp shells, you can freeze them for future use in stocks like this one.) Sear the shrimp shells, stirring occasionally, until the shells turn bright pink. Reduce the heat to low, add the vegetables, spices, and herbs, and continue to cook, stirring, for 3 to 4 more minutes. Add the tomato paste,

stirring to combine, and cook another 2 minutes. Add the wine, stir, and cook down to a glaze. Add water—just enough to cover the shells—bring up to a simmer over medium-high heat, and cook for 30 minutes. Strain stock through a fine-mesh sieve or chinois. Return the stock to the same pot. Turn the heat up to high and reduce the stock by half. Skim any fat or impurities that rise to the surface, strain once again, and set aside. (The stock stores very well frozen in an airtight container for several months.)

To make the sauce and complete the dish, preheat the broiler. Cut the tomatoes in half horizontally and place cut side down on a baking sheet. Place the sheet under the broiler and broil until the tomato skins are slightly charred and pulling away from the fruit. Cool the tomatoes and remove and discard skin. Finely chop the tomatoes and set aside. Preheat the oven to 375°F. Place 18 small bacon slabs fat side down in a single layer in a large ovenproof sauté pan. Place the pan in the oven and bake until crisped, about 15 minutes. Remove the bacon and keep warm on a foil-covered plate. Drain off all but 1 tablespoon of the bacon fat and heat the pan over medium-high heat. Add the shrimp and season with salt and pepper. Toss once or twice. When the shrimp are just turning opaque, after about 1½ minutes, add the tomatoes and toss. Add the shrimp stock, increase heat to high, and bring to a simmer. Add the butter and scallions, stirring to blend. Reduce heat to low until ready to serve.

To serve, spoon 1 to 1¼ cups of grits into six shallow bowls and scatter with bacon. Top each with the shrimp and tomato sauce. Serve immediately. This dish can also be served from a large platter.

Old Village Post House

101 Pitt Street, Mount Pleasant
(843) 388-8935 or toll free (800) 549-POST
www.oldvillageposthouse.com
Chef de Cuisine: Jim Walker

On a quiet street in the heart of Mount Pleasant's Mayberry-esque Old Village, a few doors down from a retro pharmacy that serves milkshakes and grilled cheese sandwiches at the counter, resides the Old Village Post House. A functioning inn with six guest rooms, the charming old house was originally an overnight stop for nineteenth-century horseback-riding mailmen. The Post House just oozes neighborhood charm and looks the inviting part with old-world bead board, soft earthy colors, and silent paddle fans working their meditative magic overhead.

A former member of the Air Force, who once worked the line at an enlisted dining hall that served a thousand meals five times a day, oversees the small open kitchen with pragmatism and culinary panache honed under Frank Lee at Slightly North of Broad (see page 160). Chef de cuisine Jim Walker subscribes to the basic formula of all the Maverick Southern Kitchens properties (the restaurant group also owns High Cotton, Slightly North of Broad, and High Hammock on Pawley's Island), which he describes as "Southern/Lowcountry with a twist." He personalizes the recipes on the fish- and steak-intensive menu with his commanding sense of what works best in each dish. He reworked a recipe for the restaurant's shrimp and grits, for example, to include country ham, Cajun seasoning, and andouille sausage. "The spiciness develops as you eat it. It starts on the front of the tongue and slowly moves back," says Jim of his stunningly delicious take on shrimp and grits.

LOWCOUNTRY SHRIMP AND GRITS

(Serves 4 to 6)

For the grits:

8 cups water
3 cups stone-ground grits
1 stick (¼ pound) unsalted butter
1–1½ cups heavy cream
Salt and freshly ground black pepper to taste

For the shrimp sauce:

2 tablespoons vegetable oil
1¾ pounds Thibodeaux's andouille sausage
   (or substitute another brand), cut into
   approximately 28 ½-inch-thick slices
1 cup cubed country ham (cut into ¼-inch dice)
1¼ pounds large (21–25 count) shrimp, peeled
   and deveined
½ cup finely chopped peeled and seeded tomatoes
¼ cup finely sliced scallions
4 teaspoons minced garlic
4 teaspoons Cajun-style fish blackening seasoning
   (Jim suggests R.L. Schreiber brand)
1 cup salt-free chicken stock
4 tablespoons unsalted butter
Salt and freshly ground black pepper to taste

To prepare the grits, bring the water to a boil over high heat in a large heavy-bottomed pot. Add the grits, stir, and bring back to a boil, stirring constantly with a whisk or flat-tipped wooden spoon to prevent sticking. Continue cooking on low heat, stirring, until thickened (the grits should plop like a thick cornbread batter), 30 to 40 minutes. Turn off the burner and let stand covered, so that the grits can continue to slowly absorb the water, for 1 to 2 hours. Just before serving, reheat the grits over medium heat, stirring, for about 5 minutes. Add the butter and the heavy cream, stirring to incorporate. Heat through and season to taste with salt and pepper.

Meanwhile, about 20 minutes before serving, prepare the shrimp sauce. Heat the oil over high heat in a large deep sauté pan. When hot and sizzling, add the sausage and country ham. Sauté, tossing, until the sausage and ham begin to turn golden and caramelize, about 5 minutes. Reduce the heat to medium-high. Add the shrimp, tomato, scallions, minced garlic, and Cajun-style fish blackening seasoning. Sauté for another 3 minutes, being sure to combine well and coat the ingredients evenly with the seasoning. Add the chicken stock, increase the heat to high, and cook for 1 minute. Stir in the butter and cook until the shrimp are cooked through, another 1 to 2 minutes. Season to taste with salt and pepper.

To serve, ladle the grits into shallow bowls and top with the sauce. Serve immediately.

Beef, Lamb, Pork, and More

Charleston chefs take meat and potatoes to new heights and go crazy for artisanally raised livestock from local farmers. McCrady's innovative leader, Sean Brock, raises his own pigs, which he lovingly converts into charcuterie at the esteemed restaurant. He introduces us to the velvety texture of rack of lamb coddled by sous vide's gentle embrace and pairs it with playful braised pine nuts and golden raisins. Mr. Steak himself, Oak Steakhouse's Brett McKee, slathers his New York strip with a Cajun crawfish compound butter, while Old Firehouse's Bill Twaler spreads fat pork chops with an audacious layer of house-made pimiento cheese. Out in the resort lands of Kiawah and Seabrook Islands, Matt Bolus braises beef short ribs in Guinness and fresh tangerine juice at Red Sky, and Ocean Room Prime's Nathan Thurston drizzles childish tater tots with grown-up caviar, serving them alongside grass-fed beef rib-eye steaks. Nate Whiting's long-braised pork belly melts into perfection with a Dijon mustard and espresso-infused sauce at the Dining Room at the Woodlands.

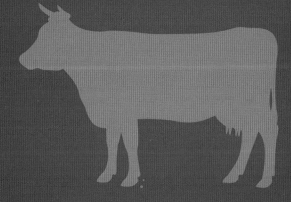

McCrady's

2 Unity Alley, downtown
(843) 577-0025
www.mccradysrestaurant.com
Executive Chef: Sean Brock

If job satisfaction plays a prominent role in life expectancy, Sean Brock will live a very, very long time. The 2008 and 2009 James Beard Rising Star Chef nominee talks about his restaurant, cooking, farming, raising pigs, protein's reaction to heat, heirloom seeds, and house-made charcuterie with the same beaming pride and love with which a father speaks of his child. And he knows what he's talking about. A staunch proponent of sous vide (see sidebar, page 149) and slow cooking, he and his staff also tend a biodynamic garden on two-and-a-half acres of land on nearby Wadmalaw Island, from which he culls produce for the restaurant and heirloom seeds to preserve dying breeds. As if that weren't enough, Sean also farms pigs that he personally converts into bacon, ham, and charcuterie—prepared, cured, and served at McCrady's.

"Our garden writes our menu. Spending time out there, hoeing onions, I smell them and all I can think about is how I'm going to cook them later that evening," says Sean with endearing enthusiasm. His combination of razor-sharp classical technique and contemporary whimsy has turned restaurant critics' and patrons' heads across the country.

McCrady's is something of an old soul, situated in what was once a public house (circa 1788) where George Washington came to dinner on a visit to Charleston during the Revolutionary War. The original heart pine floors and softened antique brick edges echo with whispers of the past, even as Sean fixes his gastronomic gaze entirely on the future, making heavenly food that's also kind to the planet.

Roasted Rack of Lamb with Salsify, Braised Pine Nuts, and Golden Raisins
(Serves 4)

For the lamb:

2 racks of American lamb, 8 bones each
3 tablespoons olive oil
Salt and freshly ground black pepper to taste
1 sprig fresh rosemary

For the salsify:

4 stalks salsify root
6 tablespoons milk
Salt and freshly ground black pepper

For the garnishes and to finish:

1 cup golden raisins
1 cup fresh-squeezed orange juice
1½ cups pine nuts
3 cups sodium-free chicken stock
3 tablespoons butter
Salt and freshly ground black pepper to taste
1 tablespoon canola oil
1 tablespoon butter

Special equipment: a pressure cooker

Rub the lamb with the olive oil and salt and pepper. Place both racks, along with the rosemary, in a Cryovac bag (see sidebar, right, for an alternative) and seal. Fill a Dutch oven or large deep pot one-quarter full with cold water and bring up to precisely 135°F over low heat. (Use a candy thermometer to regulate the heat throughout the cooking process.) Cook the lamb for exactly 12 minutes. While it's cooking, fill a large bowl with ice and cold water. When the lamb has cooked, immediately submerge it in the ice water bath. Refrigerate until ready to serve (The lamb can be stored this way for 2 to 3 days.)

To prepare the salsify, bring a medium pot of water up to a rolling boil. Peel the salsify and rinse under cold water. Place the salsify, milk, and salt and pepper in a Cryovac bag and seal. Cook in boiling water for 5 minutes. Shock by submerging in a water bath, as you did with the lamb, and refrigerate until ready to serve. (Like the lamb, the salsify can be stored for 2 to 3 days before serving.)

About 1½ hours before you're ready to serve, prepare the raisins and pine nuts. Combine the raisins and orange juice in a medium pot and cook over low heat for 30 minutes, or until the raisins are soft and plump. Puree together until smooth and strain through a fine-mesh sieve to drain any excess liquid. Set the raisin puree aside. Meanwhile, place the pine nuts, chicken stock, butter, and salt and pepper in an electric pressure cooker and cook on low pressure for 90 minutes.

To assemble the dish, heat 1 tablespoon canola oil over high heat in a large sauté pan. Sear the lamb on both sides, for 1 to 2 minutes each, or until it has a golden finish and is warmed through. Remove from the pan and let rest for 2 minutes. Meanwhile, heat 1 tablespoon butter over high heat in a medium sauté pan and add the salsify. Sauté until golden brown, about 5 minutes. To serve, slice the lamb between the bones to create 16 chops. Place approximately 3 tablespoons of the pine nut

mixture in the center of each plate. Top with a fan of 4 lamb chops. Cut the salsify stalks into 1-inch pieces and distribute alongside the lamb. Place a generous dollop of raisin puree on each plate and serve.

SOUS VIDE

Sous vide is a method of cooking developed in France that seals ingredients in vacuum-packed bags. The food is then cooked over very low heat in a temperature-controlled water bath and rapidly cooled to stop the cooking. Many chefs, like Sean, believe that this method of cooking ensures ultimate taste and texture integrity. He uses Cryovac-brand sealing bags at the restaurant, but at home you can cheat effectively by wrapping each individual cut of lamb very tightly in several layers of plastic wrap and tying off the ends with a string or rubber band to prevent water from leaking in.

Oak Steakhouse

17 Broad Street, downtown
(843) 722-4220
WWW.OAKSTEAKHOUSERESTAURANT.COM
Chef-Owner: Brett McKee

Brett McKee is the kind of guy whose personality somehow enters a room even before he does. A big, booming, no-nonsense type, so too is the hearty, sophisticated steak and Italian fare served at Oak, a dreamily beautiful nineteenth-century bank morphed into a dining destination extraordinaire.

The restaurant begins on a casual ground level, then ascends via a grand staircase, past a middle-level dining area, to the butter yellow and muted blue elegance of the top-tier dining room. No matter what the level, USDA prime beef and certified Angus are Oak's star attractions. A seasoned and successful restaurateur, Brett looks at food and cooking very simply. "Meat and potatoes are not going out of style. Froths, foams, and fusions, I don't know how long they'll be around. This is the kind of stuff I like to eat. If I like to eat it, I'm going to cook it better," says the Brooklyn native.

Whether it's the whopper 36-ounce rib-eye or the more petite filet mignon, nearly every steak at Oak gets rubbed down with a special blend of cocoa beans, espresso, salt, garlic, fennel, and more. McKee does the same thing with the Cajun Blackened New York Strip here, but refused to divulge the exact recipe for his Tuscan rub. He suggests personalizing your own rub, beginning with salt, pepper, and garlic and building it from there. Or just substitute Cajun seasoning to reflect the New Orleans–inspired flavors of this dish. At Oak, the meat is paired with classic steakhouse sides like creamed spinach, roasted beets, and hash browns and topped with chunky crawfish butter, which melts into every bite.

Cajun Blackened New York Strip with Creole Crawfish Compound Butter

(Serves 4)

For the compound butter:

2 sticks (½ pound) unsalted butter, at room temperature
½ cup finely chopped fresh crawfish, cooked
¼ cup very finely chopped fresh parsley
4 scallions, finely chopped on the bias
2 tablespoons Cajun seasoning
1 clove garlic, minced

For the steak:

1 pound white oak wood chips (or hickory or your wood of choice)
½ cup Cajun seasoning
Salt and freshly ground black pepper to taste
4 16-ounce New York strip steaks
¼ cup blended oil (3 tablespoons canola oil and 1 tablespoon extra-virgin olive oil)
2 sticks (½ pound) unsalted butter, at room temperature
4 whole cooked crawfish for garnish

A day before serving, prepare the crawfish compound butter. In the bowl of a food processor, whip the butter until smooth, about 30 seconds. All at once, add the crawfish, parsley, and scallions. Process another 10 seconds and then incorporate the Cajun seasoning and garlic, pulsing another 2 or 3 times to blend. Turn butter out onto a large square of waxed paper. Fold the waxed paper over the top of the butter and begin rolling so the butter forms a log about the diameter of a quarter. Wrap the log tightly in the waxed paper and refrigerate overnight. (The butter can be prepared 2 to 3 days in advance.)

On grilling day, soak the wood chips in a large bowl of cold water for at least 2 hours. Heat a gas grill to medium-high. Drain the wood chips, place them in a large flat pan off to the side of the grilling surface, and close the grill top. If using a charcoal grill, place the soaked wood chips directly on top of hot coals, add the grill, and cover. Wait for the chips to start smoking, about 15 minutes. Remember to keep the grill top closed to retain the smoky flavor.

Combine the Cajun seasoning with salt and pepper and coat each of the steaks heavily and completely with the mixture. Once the wood chips are smoking, carefully brush the grill surface with the blended oil. Place the steaks on the grill on the diagonal, evenly spacing them. To create beautiful grill marks, cook for 2 to 3 minutes and then turn the steaks one-quarter turn, to an opposite angle. Cook for an additional 2 to 3 minutes and flip the steaks, repeating cooking on the other side until medium rare. (Medium rare generally has an internal temperature between 130–140°F. This can be tested with a meat thermometer.) Remove the steaks from the grill and brush both sides with the soft butter. Let rest on a large platter for 5 minutes.

To finish, heat a large cast-iron pan over high heat. Place the steaks (in batches if necessary) in the pan and sear for 20 seconds, flip, and repeat

on the other side. Serve each steak with a slice or two of the crawfish butter, cut into ¼-inch-thick rounds, on top and garnish each with a whole crawfish.

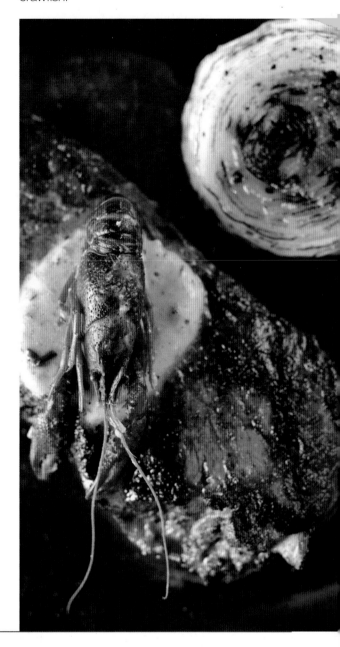

THE DINING ROOM AT WOODLANDS

125 PARSONS ROAD, SUMMERVILLE
(843) 875-2600 OR TOLL FREE (800) 774-9999
WWW.WOODLANDSINN.COM
EXECUTIVE CHEF: NATE WHITING

A long string of highly decorated chefs, from Lucca's Ken Vedrinski to the Georgian Room's Scott Crawford (at the Cloister at Sea Island), preceded Nate Whiting to the executive chef post at this storied Mobil Five-Star restaurant and inn. But that doesn't scare the thirty-year-old. "I'm inspired by the challenge. I always strive to do my best and not compromise the quality of anything," says Nate.

Indeed, excellence permeates the place, situated on sprawling grounds in a gracious nineteenth-century home-turned-inn, complete with rocking chairs on the front porch and beefed up with the spotless reputation of relatively new owner Salamander Hospitality. The dining room itself is a soothing oasis of Southern gentility, subdued charm, and refined service by a largely European staff, including Frenchman and Master Sommelier Stephane Peltier, who expertly navigates clients through the restaurant's 1,000-deep wine list.

In addition to top-quality ingredients, Nate likes to unify his creations with a theme. While

one dish may use all parts of a plant—saffron (stamens), cinnamon (bark), and star anise (fruit)—another marries apricot and lavender, "because lavender grows under apricot trees," Nate explains.

It's a poetic way of looking at things, so it's not surprising that Whiting's food is the culinary equivalent of soul-stirring poetry. The following dish showcases Berkshire pork, a specialty breed. If it's unavailable, Whiting suggests substituting an artisanal pork product purchased from a local farmer. The pork is brined and braised before it's crisped in a pan and served with a simple white bean puree and earthy Dijon mustard–espresso sauce. Nate insists on measuring ingredients by weight for precision and consistency, so weights in grams are provided here along with volume equivalents. To cook by weight, Nate suggests buying an inexpensive digital scale at a specialty cooking shop for priceless results.

Crispy Berkshire Pork Belly with White Bean Puree and Dijon Mustard and Espresso Sauce

(Serves 6)

For the brine:

4 liters (1 gallon) cold water
360g (1¼ cups) sea salt
475g (2 cups) granulated sugar
25g (2 tablespoons) yellow mustard seeds, wrapped in a cheesecloth pouch
5 fresh bay leaves or 3 dry bay leaves
2 Vidalia onions (or other sweet onions), halved and charred cut side down in a hot pan
1 head of garlic, halved and charred cut side down in a hot pan
3 sprigs fresh thyme
2kg (about 4 pounds) Berkshire skin-on pork belly

For the white bean puree:

325g (3 cups) dried Great Northern beans
7g (½ teaspoon) sea salt
Generous pinch of dark roast ground espresso (Nate suggests Illy brand)
18g (2 tablespoons) Banyuls vinegar or sherry vinegar
2g (¼ teaspoon) fresh-squeezed lemon juice
60g (¼ cup) heavy cream
90g (5 tablespoons) butter

To braise and finish the pork:

2 Vidalia onions (or other sweet onions), halved and charred cut side down in a hot pan
1 head garlic, halved and charred cut side down in a hot pan
3 sprigs fresh thyme
1 liter (about 1 quart) canola oil or vegetable oil, or enough to cover

For the sauce:

155g (¾ cup) Dijon mustard
65g (¼ cup) extra-virgin olive oil
5g (½ teaspoon) fresh-squeezed lemon juice
5g (1 tablespoon) finely chopped chives
Generous pinch of dark roast ground espresso (Nate suggests Illy brand)
Salt and freshly ground black pepper to taste
Ground espresso for garnish (optional)

Three days before serving, prepare the brine. Combine 1 liter of water, the salt, and the sugar in a large pot and bring up to a boil to dissolve the solids. Add the remaining cold water and other ingredients, except the pork belly. Cool the mixture completely in the refrigerator. Pour into a nonreactive (glass or ceramic) container, and submerge the pork belly. Cover and store in the refrigerator for 3 days.

Two days before serving, prepare the beans. Rinse the beans thoroughly and place them in a large bowl, covered with cold water. Soak overnight. The following day, drain the beans and place them in a large, broad ovenproof pot or a Dutch oven. Cover with water and bring to a lively simmer over medium-high heat on the stove. Preheat the oven to 325°F. Cover the pot and place the pot in the oven. Cook until the beans are very soft, about 2 hours. Check every 30 minutes to see if more water is needed; the beans need to swim in broth to cook.

To finish the beans, drain the beans when soft, reserving 200g (about 2 cups) of the cooking liquid. Puree the beans and reserved liquid with the remaining puree ingredients until silky smooth. The puree should be thick enough to eat with a fork. If it seems too thick, add a little more reserved cooking liquid or water. Pass puree through a fine-mesh strainer, pressing with a wooden spoon or ladle, into a glass or ceramic bowl. Clean the strainer and pass the puree through again. Taste and adjust salt as needed. Set aside. (Note: The beans can be prepared a day before the pork is braised, seared, and served.)

On the day of service, the third day, return to the pork. Preheat oven to 300°F. Remove the pork belly from the brine and pat dry. Discard the brine. Place the pork belly, onion, garlic, and thyme sprigs in an ovenproof pan. Pour in the liter of canola or vegetable oil to cover the pork belly, using more or less as needed. Cover pan with aluminum foil and cook the pork in the oven until it is fork-tender, 3 to 4 hours.

On the third day, the day of service, prepare the Dijon mustard sauce. Whisk together all of the ingredients in a medium bowl to form a uniform emulsion.

By now, the pork should be nearly ready to finish and serve. When it's completely cooked, remove the onion, garlic, and thyme from the pan and allow the pork belly to cool in its cooking oil. When cool, remove the pork belly from the pan and wipe off any coagulated fat with a clean kitchen towel or paper towels. Slice the pork into ½-inch-thick squares, counting on about 4 slices per person. (You may have some left over, which can be crisped off over the next several days and used in another dish.) Preheat the oven to 350°F. Heat a large nonstick sauté pan over high heat. Place the pork belly slices skin side down in the pan and cook quickly (about 2 minutes) in the sauté pan on the stovetop, until the skin is just crisped. Pour in enough Dijon mustard sauce to just coat the pork and heat the sauce-glazed pork still in the sauté pan. Remove the sauté pan from the oven and place in the oven, heating through for about 15 minutes. Separately, reheat the white bean puree over low heat in a medium saucepan, stirring.

To serve, place a generous dollop of the white bean puree in the center of each plate and top with 4 slices of the crisped pork belly. If desired, garnish with a pinch of ground espresso beans.

Ocean Room Prime

One Sanctuary Beach Drive, Kiawah Island
(843) 768-6253
WWW.KIAWAHRESORT.COM
Chef de Cuisine: Nathan Thurston

During the forty-five-minute drive from downtown to this breathtakingly beautiful barrier island, stress melts palpably away, like cold butter on a slow, easy simmer. The road weaves through arches of live oaks and marshes dappled with a dizzying dance of light swaying playfully with shade. By the time you're there, the vacation's begun, and Ocean Room Prime is the place to spend it.

The fanciest and priciest of the tony resort's five restaurants, it is also the most beautiful, draped with swath upon swath of hand-wrought iron depicting marsh scenes and wildlife. The Mobil Four Star and AAA Four Diamond restaurant sits atop a sweeping staircase—think Scarlett and Rhett's posh Atlanta pad in *Gone with the Wind*.

Ironically enough, Prime specializes in alternatives to prime beef. Most of the beef on the menu is grass-fed and (like the pork and the chicken) comes from hand-selected ranchers within 100 miles of the restaurant.

Nathan describes his hand-crafted menu as "contemporary American cuisine sourcing local products." At Ocean Room Prime, the seasons dictate all the sides, such as roasted seasonal mushrooms and à la minute mashed potatoes cooked to order. And for all his serious talk about grass-fed beef and local sourcing, Nathan has lots of creative fun with his food, in whimsical dishes like Lobster Bisque with Lobster Salad and Tarragon Marshmallows and the rib-eye recipe below.

Nathan says he can't overstate the importance of resting when working with grass-fed beef. If the meat isn't rested at least 10 or 15 minutes, he says, you'll "miss out on the pureness that can be there." Look for grass-fed beef at your local farmers' market. ("Mibek" in this recipe name refers to a Charleston-area farmer.)

Grilled Mibek Farms Rib-Eye with Tater Tots and Caviar
(Serves 4)

For the tater tots:

2 pounds Idaho potatoes, well scrubbed
1 tablespoon olive oil
1 leek, well washed and minced
1 tablespoon melted butter
Salt and freshly ground black pepper to taste
1 cup all-purpose flour
4 eggs, beaten
1 cup panko bread crumbs
1–2 cups canola oil, or as needed

For the steaks:

4 12-ounce grass-fed rib-eye steaks
¼ cup olive oil
Sea salt and freshly ground black pepper to taste
2 tablespoons cold butter

For the garnish:

1 tablespoon caviar
3 tablespoons crème fraîche
8 chives, cut into 1½-inch lengths

Special equipment: twenty 2-inch stainless-steel ring molds

To prepare the tater tots, preheat the oven to 375°F. Bake the potatoes for 20 minutes or until they are halfway baked and softening to the touch. Remove from the oven and let rest until they're cool enough to handle. Meanwhile, heat the olive oil in a small sauté pan over medium heat and sauté the leek until soft, about 8 minutes.

Peel the potatoes and grate on the medium-sized holes of a box grater. Combine the potatoes with the sautéed leek and the melted butter in a large bowl. Season to taste with salt and pepper. To form the tots, press the mixture into 2-inch ring molds lined up on a sheet pan and refrigerate until firm. Season the flour lightly with salt and pepper, then put the flour, the beaten eggs, and the panko in separate shallow bowls. To bread the tots, first dip in the flour, then the eggs, and finally the panko. Return the tots to the sheet pan and refrigerate while you cook the steaks.

Nathan prefers to cook grass-fed beef in a cast-iron pan, but he says a grill works fine when the weather invites outdoor cooking. Either way, generously rub each steak with olive oil and season moderately with sea salt and pepper. In a hot pan or on a hot grill, sear on both sides to rare (120–125°F) or medium rare (130–135°F), 3 to 5 minutes on each side. "Any further cooking of this cut, especially grass-fed, will dry out the steak and jeopardize its integrity," says Nathan. To finish, rub the butter on the steak and let it rest, uncovered, for 10 to 15 minutes.

Meanwhile, return to the tots. Pour ½ inch of canola oil into a deep pot over medium-high heat. When the oil has reached 325°F, place the tots in the pot, being careful to avoid splashing. Do not crowd the tater tots; fry them in batches if necessary. Fry until the tots are golden brown on all sides, about 4 minutes. Drain on paper towels.

To serve, arrange a steak on the side of each plate. Stack the tots together on a platter, serving family-style, and drizzle them with caviar and crème fraîche. Arrange the chives on top and serve immediately. My advice? Skip the ketchup!

OLD FIREHOUSE RESTAURANT

6350 HIGHWAY 162, HOLLYWOOD
(843) 889-9512
WWW.OLDFIREHOUSE.COM
CHEF-OWNER: BILL TWALER

This prime roadside find is tucked away in a virtual hamlet of a town between Charleston and Edisto, about 30 minutes from downtown. Formerly a fire station, it still has shades of its 1950s cinderblock past and is decked with dalmatian kitsch, but don't let that fool you. Bill Twaler, who refers to himself as "chief bottle washer," can really, really cook. His style is substantive and real. Liver pudding, wings, scallops with garlic butter, and seafood mac 'n' cheese are just some of his deceptively simple-sounding delicacies.

This Johnson & Wales grad, one-time safari chef in Zimbabwe, and Iowa City, Iowa, native loves to cook. "It's Bill's cuisine. It's my food. We call ourselves 'Lowcountry eclectic' because we use as many Lowcountry ingredients as possible, but at the same time, if I go have sushi somewhere with my wife on Sunday, you're probably going to see sushi here on the menu by Tuesday," Bill explains.

Pimiento cheese is big in these parts. In most places, it's served with crackers or as part of a sandwich, but Bill audaciously slathers his zesty house-made blend on top of fat porterhouse-cut pork chops he buys from a local farmer and finishes them off with a quick melting broil. At Old Firehouse, the decadent chop is served with mashed potatoes and butter-browned green cabbage. Save any leftover cheese for snacking.

PIMIENTO CHEESE CHOP
(Serves 6)

For the pimiento cheese:

2 cups grated pepper Jack cheese
2 cups grated sharp cheddar
2 cups shredded provolone
½ cup diced canned pimientos, drained
½ cup minced sweet onion (such as Vidalia)
1 cup mayonnaise
½ cup brown spicy mustard
¼ cup jalapeño Tabasco green pepper sauce

For the chops:

6 ½-inch-thick porterhouse pork chops (preferably farm-raised)
Salt and freshly ground black pepper to taste
Dusting of Cajun seasoning

To prepare the pimiento cheese, toss the cheeses with the diced pimiento and onion. Add mayonnaise and mustard and stir with a wooden spoon until smooth. Add the Tabasco and stir to combine. Set aside. (The pimiento cheese can be made up to 2 days in advance. Store covered in the refrigerator.)

Preheat the broiler. Season the chops all over with salt and pepper and dust very lightly with Cajun seasoning. Sear in a medium-hot pan or grill, 5 to 6 minutes on each side, until cooked to medium. Let rest for 10 minutes. To finish, top each chop with ¼ to ½ cup of the pimiento cheese. Spread with a knife to cover each chop evenly. Place the chops on a broiler pan and broil about 2-inches from the heating element until the cheese just begins to bubble, 1 to 2 minutes. Serve immediately and watch out!

Red Sky Grill

100 Landfall Way, Johns Island
(843) 768-0183
www.redskydining.com
Executive Chef-Owner: Matt Bolus

Vinegar and vanilla are big-time culinary hot buttons for stockbroker-turned-chef Matt Bolus. Why? Because both represent what the young cooking maestro embraces in life and in his kitchen—eco-friendliness, purity, and complexity. On vinegar Bolus says, "Necessity is the mother of invention. If I can't sell a whole bottle of wine after it's opened for a glass pouring, I use the rest to make vinegar." Bolus is committed to recycling everything he can and composting coffee grounds and tea leaves, veggies, paper scraps, and more to eliminate as much waste as possible and grow a garden for the restaurant. On vanilla, something he co-wrote a cookbook about, Bolus exclaims, "What's not to like? There are two hundred recognized flavors in vanilla."

At Red Sky, this graduate of Le Cordon Bleu London and former Ocean Room sous chef combines vanilla-seared tilapia with shiitake-infused basmati or tangerine and Guinness-braised short ribs in unorthodox yet intelligent culinary machinations.

The setting here is simple and well-suited to the laid-back tempo of Seabrook Island, which is a little more blue-collar and relaxed than beautiful yet slightly uppity Kiawah, the next island over.

How delicious does this sound?

Guinness and Tangerine Braised Beef Short Ribs with Cauliflower Puree
(Serves 6)

For the ribs:

2–3 pounds boneless beef short ribs
Salt and freshly ground black pepper to taste
2 tablespoons olive oil
2 carrots, peeled and cut into large dice
2 onions, cut into large dice
3 stalks celery, cut into large dice
4 cups veal stock (or substitute sodium-free beef or chicken stock)
1 12-ounce can Guinness
Zest of 2 tangerines
¾ cup fresh-squeezed tangerine juice
½ bunch thyme, wrapped with kitchen string, plus more for garnish (optional)
5 whole black peppercorns

For the cauliflower puree:

1 head cauliflower, quartered, cored, and coarsely chopped
2 cups heavy cream (or substitute half-and-half or 2 percent milk)
Juice of ½ lemon
Salt and freshly ground black pepper to taste

Preheat the oven to 350°F. To prepare the ribs, season the ribs with salt and pepper on all sides. Heat the olive oil in a large, heavy-bottomed pan or a Dutch oven over high heat. When the oil is hot, add the ribs in a single layer and "sear them hard" on all sides until golden. Do not move the ribs once they've hit the pan until they're golden, then turn and repeat. Remove the ribs from the pan. Reduce the heat to medium and add the carrots, onion, and celery. Cook, stirring, until the

vegetables have softened and caramelized, about 7 minutes. Return the ribs to the pan and add the stock, Guinness, tangerine zest, tangerine juice, thyme, and peppercorns. Stir, scraping the bottom of the pan to release the black bits of flavor from the searing and caramelizing process. Cover the pan, place in the oven, and cook for 3½ hours. Check every hour to make sure the cooking is even and to see how the meat is breaking down. The ribs are done when the meat is very tender and easily torn apart. Remove the ribs from the liquid and reserve, covered with foil. Strain the vegetables and other solids from the cooking liquid and discard, returning the liquid to the pan. Skim off any visible fat and reduce the liquid by half over medium-high heat, allowing it to come to a sauce consistency.

Near the end of the ribs' cooking time, prepare the cauliflower puree. Combine the cauliflower and cream in a medium pot over medium-low heat and cook until the cauliflower is very tender, 25 to 30 minutes. Drain then puree the cauliflower in a food processor with just enough of the cream to form a smooth puree. Add the cream in batches, as you may not need it all. Add lemon juice and salt and pepper to taste. Reheat the puree over low heat before serving.

To serve, place a generous dollop of the cauliflower puree on each plate, top with 2 or 3 ribs, and dress with the sauce. Garnish with fresh thyme sprigs if desired.

SLIGHTLY NORTH OF BROAD (S.N.O.B.)

192 East Bay Street, downtown
(843) 723-3424
WWW.MAVERICKSOUTHERNKITCHENS.COM
Vice President Culinary Development, Maverick Southern
Kitchens: Frank Lee

No conversation about Charleston's cuisine scene would be complete without mention of Frank Lee and his myriad groundbreaking contributions. A true titan of taste and a South Carolina native, Frank is a self-taught cook who's been cooking professionally since the early seventies and who led the elite chefs' posse in Charleston's post–Hurricane Hugo culinary maturation.

A French classical technique devotee, Frank's dressed-down toque comes in the form of a red chile pepper baseball cap. You can barely follow his bobbing, busy head as he navigates the open kitchen here, where he's taught and groomed some of Charleston's finest chefs and servers.

S.N.O.B.'s menu of contemporary Southern compositions with a strong vegetarian and ethnic leaning changes daily but maintains core favorites such as the Maverick Beef Tenderloin. "It's a take on veal Oscar. I turned it into beef with crab and béarnaise with a really good pepper sauce," says Frank. "My menu is really a composite of the people I've worked for and the people who have worked for me. I just find ways to make them (the recipes) more interesting," says the humble, hard-working chef.

S.N.O.B. is a pretty, feminine restaurant, so named because it lies just a few blocks north of Broad Street, what locals think of as the dividing line between those with means (and local bloodlines) and those with less. For the record, those who live below Broad are known as S.O.B.s, yet another example of Charlestonians' wily wit.

GRILLED MAVERICK BEEF TENDERLOIN WITH DEVILED CRAB CAKE, BÉARNAISE, AND GREEN PEPPERCORN SAUCE

(Serves 6)

For the devil crab mix:

1 pound crab claws, picked
2 tablespoons yellow mustard
¼ cup whole cream
1¼ cups cracker meal (savory crackers such as Saltines, smashed and ground)
1 egg

6 dashes Tabasco sauce
1 tablespoon fresh-squeezed lemon juice
¼ cup finely diced green or red bell pepper
¼ cup finely diced red onion
½ teaspoon salt
½ teaspoon freshly ground black pepper
1 quart vegetable oil

For the green peppercorn sauce:

1 tablespoon butter
1 small red onion, finely diced
1 teaspoon salt, plus more to taste
½ cup brandy
1 quart reduced veal stock (unsalted stock that's
    been reduced by half)
2 tablespoons green peppercorns, drained

For the béarnaise:

3 egg yolks
1 teaspoon salt
3 tablespoons water
½ cup fresh-squeezed lemon juice
2 dashes Tabasco sauce
½ bunch tarragon, stemmed and finely chopped,
    plus more for garnish (optional)
8 ounces (2 sticks) unsalted butter, at room
    temperature

For the tenderloin:

6 6- to 8-ounce beef tenderloins
Salt and freshly ground black pepper

Prepare the devil crab mix. Combine all the ingredients except 1 cup of the cracker meal and the vegetable oil in a medium bowl, mixing gently with a wooden spoon. Allow to rest at room temperature for 1 hour.

Meanwhile, prepare the green peppercorn sauce. Heat the butter, onion, and salt together over medium heat in a medium saucepan. Cook until the onion has softened, about 5 minutes. Add the brandy, increase the heat to medium-high,

and reduce the brandy to a thick glaze. Add the reduced veal stock and bring to a simmer over medium-high heat. Reduce the sauce until it's thickened and shiny, skimming off any foam with a ladle. Add peppercorns and salt to taste. Set aside.

Next, prepare the béarnaise. Remember, this is an emulsion sauce, so temperature is important to prevent the sauce from breaking. Make this just before you grill the steak and cook the crab cakes, and keep it warm (at 145°F) for a few minutes at room temperature or for longer over a gentle water bath. To make the sauce, combine the egg yolks, salt, and water in a mixing bowl. Place over a pot of boiling water and whisk until the eggs begin to thicken and the sauce temperature reaches 145°F. Remove from the heat. Add lemon juice, Tabasco, and tarragon. Return the sauce to the water bath or heat and whisk until all ingredients are incorporated. Add the butter, 1 tablespoon at a time, whisking constantly, to create a thick and fluffy sauce. Set aside.

Form the crab cakes into 3-ounce patties and dust in the remaining 1 cup of cracker meal. Heat the oil to 350°F in a large pot over medium-high heat. Fry the cakes until they're golden brown all over, 3 to 5 minutes. Remove and drain on paper towels. Season lightly with salt.

Heat the grill to medium high. Season the tenderloin with salt and pepper. When the grill is hot, grill meat to desired doneness and remove from the grill. Let it rest 5 to 10 minutes.

To assemble the dish, reheat the sauces if necessary. Dress each plate with a few spoonfuls of green peppercorn sauce. Place tenderloin in the center of each plate and top with a hot crab cake. Top this with a few spoonfuls of warm béarnaise. Dress each plate with a sprig of fresh tarragon if desired.

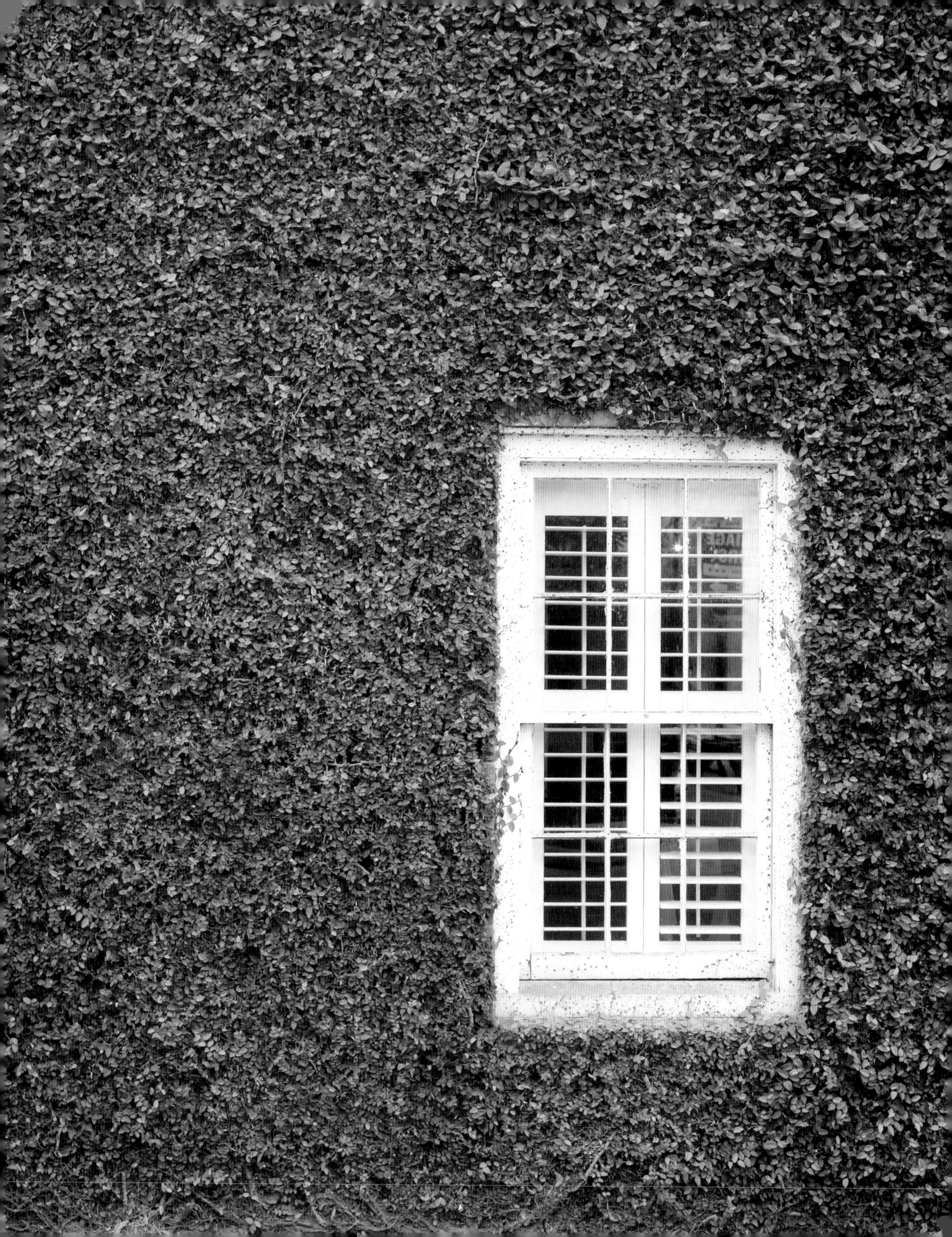

POULTRY PERCH

Birds of all feathers have long flocked together in Lowcountry kitchens. Chicken, an affordable and broadly interpreted ingredient in the South and in Charleston, is perhaps most beloved in its slyly simple form—fried. James Beard Award winner Robert Stehling treats his buttermilk-soaked birds to a bath of spiced peach gravy at Hominy Grill, while the Grant sisters at Bertha's Kitchen are so secretive they don't dare share their recipe. However, they generously offer some covert fried chicken tips. Meanwhile, chicken heads south of the border with Santiago Zavalza's sunny take on Pollo Mole Verde at Santi's.

When autumn's chill eases into Charleston's usually balmy air, around late October, camouflage clothing and gun gear emerge like so many birds heading south for winter. Duck, geese, quail, and other fowl start showing up on restaurant menus in inventive preparations like Jeremiah Bacon's glazed quail served with classic Southern staples—collard greens, bacon, hominy, and black-eyed pea relish. Robert's of Charleston's MariElana Raya gives roast breast of duckling a French twist with a splash of butternut squash sauce and a bed of butternut squash risotto.

Hominy Grill

207 Rutledge Avenue, downtown
(843) 937-0930
www.hominygrill.com
Chef-Owner: Robert Stehling

Robert Stehling is a perfect amalgamation of his cooking-intensive childhood in Greensboro, North Carolina, his professional experience, and his artistic, beat-of-his-own-drummer personality. As a kid, he canned and preserved produce from his family's huge organic garden, getting close to food and his Southern roots. Later, the UNC art major needed a job and picked up an apron and sponge to wash dishes at the celebrated Crook's Corner in Chapel Hill. "It was unbelievable there. All the dishwashers had PhDs. It was almost like a commune. There was a fabulous focus on Southern food there," says Robert. Six years later, he "turned loose" and made a working tour of some of Manhattan's best restaurants before coming down to Charleston to open Hominy Grill.

Mostly known for its hearty, Southern breakfasts and sturdy working lunches, Hominy also puts out stunning dinners in its quiet single-house setting on the medical side of town. After years of accolades, Robert achieved one of the highest kinds of praise, receiving the James Beard Best Southeastern Chef award in 2008, something that he sincerely says "surprised" him a little. Considering that this man can make something as simple as squash casserole or mac 'n' cheese taste like fresh descents from heaven and biscuits so high and light they practically touch it, this happy news should have come as no surprise at all. This is some of the best food you can eat in Charleston or in the South. Don't even get me started on the chocolate pudding or buttermilk pie. In the recipe that follows, Robert sticks with Del Monte spiced canned peaches for "something extra." They can be found in most grocery stores in the South.

Fried Chicken with Spiced Peach Gravy
(Serves 5 to 6)

For the fried chicken:

1 3- to 3½-pound chicken
1 cup buttermilk
2 cups peanut oil
1 cup all-purpose flour
2 teaspoons salt
2 teaspoons freshly ground black pepper

For the spiced peach gravy:

2 tablespoons butter
¼ cup minced onion
2 tablespoons all-purpose flour
Salt and freshly ground black pepper, to taste
1 cup chicken stock
½ cup Del Monte spiced peaches, chopped
¼–½ cup syrup from the canned peaches

Special equipment: a large cast-iron skillet

Cut the chicken into 8 evenly sized pieces, leaving the bones in and the skin intact. Place the chicken and the buttermilk in a large bowl, toss to coat, and marinate for at least 2 hours. Heat the oil over medium-high heat in a large cast-iron skillet. Combine the flour and the salt and pepper in a paper bag and drop the chicken into the bag, tossing to coat evenly. Shake off any excess flour and begin to fry the chicken, starting with the dark pieces, then following with the white pieces. Reduce the heat to medium, cover the skillet, and fry 15 minutes. Remove the cover, turn each piece of chicken over, and fry, uncovered, for another 10 to 15 minutes. Remove the chicken carefully with tongs and drain on paper towels.

Meanwhile, make the gravy. Drain and discard all but 1 tablespoon of the oil used for frying. Heat the skillet over medium heat and add the butter and onion. Cook, stirring, until the onion is golden, about 5 minutes. Lightly season the flour with salt and pepper, then whisk it into the gravy and cook, stirring, until golden brown. Whisk in the chicken stock, bring to a boil over high heat, and whisk until thickened slightly. Add the peaches and the syrup to the skillet and reduce the heat to low. Simmer for 4 to 5 minutes. Season to taste with salt and pepper.

To serve, put a piece or two of chicken on each plate and top with a generous amount of peach gravy. The chicken is excellent with home-style mashed potatoes.

Cypress

167 East Bay Street, downtown
(843) 727-0111
www.magnolias-blossom-cypress.com
Executive Chef: Craig Deihl

Craig Deihl was just twenty-three years old in 2001 when he assumed the head role at the Hospitality Group's premier restaurant property, Cypress. He admits with his signature candor that his culinary personality was still evolving at the time. Indeed, then more retro and clubbish, dishing out classics like chateaubriand and tableside Caesar salads, these days Cypress and Craig are all grown up, serving new-world, classically interpreted Lowcountry creations in the restaurant's old-world, nineteenth-century warehouse setting.

The restaurant's stunning and dramatic interior—which houses a wall of wine and features a bird's-eye view of the spacious kitchen from a sophisticated upstairs bar—is the perfect backdrop to Craig's goodies, from house-made, grass-fed beef and local pork pepperonis and hams to the local, seasonal produce he weaves into his edible bag of tricks. Craig likes to build dishes that utilize the entire palate—hot, salty, bitter—to create memorable taste parades, as in the recipe that follows. "Colorful and piquant, this chicken recipe is a nice way to show off with exotic blood oranges. They have a deeper flavor than traditional oranges and are commonly available in produce sections during the fall and early winter season," says Craig.

Pan-Roasted Chicken with Baby Beets, Artichokes, and Blood Orange Vinaigrette
(Serves 4)

For the vinaigrette:

¼ cup fresh-squeezed blood orange juice
¼ cup sherry vinegar
1 tablespoon minced shallot
2 tablespoons honey
4 tablespoons extra-virgin olive oil
1½ teaspoons salt
Pinch of white pepper
1 tablespoon minced chives

For the artichokes:

¼ cup fresh-squeezed lemon juice
4 cups water
10 cocktail artichokes (about 1 pound)
Fresh basil, thyme, and tarragon sprigs (3 each)
¼ cup white wine
2 tablespoons salt
½ teaspoon white pepper

For the beets:

6 baby (golf ball–sized) beets
2 tablespoons olive oil
2 tablespoons white wine vinegar
2 teaspoons salt
Pinch of white pepper

For the chicken:

4 boneless chicken breasts
Salt and white pepper to taste
¼ cup canola oil, or as needed
3 tablespoons butter
1 tablespoon finely chopped thyme leaves
4 chive tips, for garnish

Begin with the vinaigrette. In a small mixing bowl, combine all of the ingredients except the minced chives, and whisk. Refrigerate, covered, until ready to use. (The vinaigrette can be prepared a day ahead.)

Next, prepare the artichokes. In a medium saucepan, combine the lemon juice and water. Peel away the outer leaves of the artichokes. Place the artichokes on a cutting board and cut the top of the artichoke, where the leaves start to change from yellow to green, about ½ inch from the top. Peel the stems and trim away the firm green skin with a paring knife. Place the artichokes in the lemon water. Wrap a couple sprigs of each herb with kitchen string, creating a little herb bundle (bouquet garni). Add the bouquet garni, the white wine, and salt and pepper to the saucepan. Place pan over medium heat and bring to a simmer. Cook for 35 minutes or until the artichokes are fork-tender. Remove from heat and allow the artichokes to cool in the liquid. Remove the bouquet garni and discard. Slice the artichokes in half vertically and return to the liquid. Set aside.

To prepare the beets, preheat the oven to 350°F. Place the beets on a large sheet of aluminum foil and mix with the remaining ingredients, tossing to coat. Wrap the foil around the beets to form a tight package, making sure there are no openings in the foil pack. Place on a sheet pan and roast for about 45 minutes, depending on the actual size of the beets. They are done when they are fork-tender. Remove from the oven, carefully open the foil pack to release steam, and allow the beets to cool. Drain any juice and reserve for when the beets are reheated. Use a rubbing motion with a clean kitchen towel to pry the skin loose from the beets. (Craig recommends wearing gloves to prevent the juice from turning fingers pink.) Slice the stem off each beet and cut into quarters.

To prepare the chicken, season the chicken breasts on both sides with salt and pepper. Place a large sauté pan over medium heat and add the oil to a depth of ⅛ inch. Heat until the oil is hot and starting to move around in the pan. Carefully lay the chicken breasts skin side down in the pan. Cook for 4 minutes, reduce heat to medium-low, and cook for 5 more minutes. Turn the chicken and cook for 6 minutes on the second side. Add the butter and thyme to the pan and baste the chicken with the juices, using a spoon, for a full 2 minutes. The chicken should be done at this point: the juices will run clear and it will have an internal temperature of 160°F. Remove from the pan and place the chicken on clean kitchen towels. Allow to rest for 5 minutes.

To finish the dish, whisk the remaining chives into room-temperature vinaigrette. Reheat the beets over low heat in a saucepan with their reserved juices and gently reheat the artichokes in their cooking juice for 5 minutes, over medium-low heat. Slice the chicken into 1-inch-thick slices on the bias just before serving. To plate, place a combination of beets and artichokes alongside a pool of the vinaigrette. Top with the sliced chicken breast and garnish each with a chive tip.

SANTI'S RESTAURANTE MEXICANO

1302 MEETING STREET ROAD, UPTOWN CHARLESTON
(843) 722-2633
114 HOLIDAY DRIVE, SUMMERVILLE
(843) 851-2885
OWNERS: JEFF HEFEL AND SANTIAGO ZAVALZA

No matter how hard you try, it is virtually impossible not to reorder the same thing you had the first time you entered Santi's flawlessly flavorful realm. It's like the first love you'll never forget and to whom no one else can compare. For me, it's the mole and verde sauces, but everybody has their own Santi's love story.

Something of a sleeper when the original location opened on a lonely end of Meeting Street Road in 2004, Santi's quickly became a local favorite for exceptional and authentic Mexican food prepared by Mexico native Santiago Zavalza. "You need to know the flavors and how things are supposed to cook to do it right. And, no shortcuts!" he explains. Whole fresh chickens are poached in huge pots with a head of garlic and a whole onion for Santi's flavorful chicken, which is served with a mole verde sauce that pops with peppery pungency.

Former agricultural engineer and substitute teacher Jeff Hefel applies his mathematical mind to balancing the books and his natural affability at the front of the small house, overseeing the lively crowd of bankers, bikers, and other assorted types who regularly flock to the restaurant.

At Santi's, the chicken is paired with Spanish rice, black beans, fat avocado slices, and corn tortillas. The chicken is also excellent wrapped up in a soft tortilla, topped with the sauce and cheese, and heated in the oven for a winning enchilada.

POLLO MOLE VERDE (CHICKEN IN GREEN SAUCE)
(Serves 4–6)

6 chicken leg quarters, skin on
5 garlic cloves
½ yellow onion
3 16-ounce cans tomatillos, well drained
6 whole jalapeños
3 chicken bouillon cubes
Freshly ground black pepper to taste
3 tablespoons vegetable oil
Salt to taste

Place the chicken in a large pot and add water to cover. Add 3 of the garlic cloves and the onion and bring to a boil over high heat. Then reduce to a simmer and cook until the chicken is tender and cooked through, about 40 minutes. When the chicken is done, drain it well and set aside. When cool enough to handle, pull the chicken from the bones in long, thick shreds. Discard the bones and skin.

To make the sauce, combine the tomatillos, jalapeños, 2 garlic cloves, bouillon cubes, and a pinch of black pepper in the bowl of a food processor or blender. Blend until chunky-smooth, about 2 minutes. Set aside.

Heat the oil in a large, deep pan over medium-high heat. When hot, add the sauce and the chicken. Reduce the heat to low and simmer gently for about 10 minutes or until hot throughout. Season to taste with salt and pepper. Serve hot with Santi's favorite garnishes, as suggested above, or use some of your own favorites..

Carolina's Southern Bistro

10 Exchange Street, downtown
(843) 724-3800
WWW.CAROLINASRESTAURANT.COM
Executive Chef: Jeremiah Bacon

Ten years working at celebrated kitchens in New York and Boston and a trek around Europe proved to be an invaluable educational investment for Charleston native Jeremiah Bacon. With stints at Per Se and Le Bernadin (among others), Jeremiah learned from the best.

Bacon—and who doesn't love that name for a chef?—grew up on a remote stretch of Johns Island, crabbing, fishing, and cooking with his grandmother and mother. "I love to eat. I had a great pimiento cheese sandwich for lunch an hour ago and I'm already thinking about what I'm going to eat for dinner," exclaims Bacon.

He applies his zeal with aplomb at Carolina's, a long-standing Charleston institution that's had its share of temporary losing streaks, converted to a long winning streak when Jeremiah took over four years ago. His restrained, delicate, and refined style draws on classical technique and contemporary interpretations of Southern food. The relaxed, sexy style of the actual space influences the food, too. Sophisticated Perdita's Room, the comfortable bar, and the family-style Sidewalk Room evoke three distinct moods. "The flexibility of the upscale bistro menu allows me to come up with food that's appropriate to every room," Jeremiah says.

The following dish is an excellent example of Jeremiah's culinary mission. "The collards are cut into a pretty chiffonade and given a quick sauté with fat from the bacon. They are tender and brilliant green in color and served on a hominy puree with a black-eyed pea relish. It's quite elegant to look at and it eats very well," he says. Indeed, it's all that and more.

Glazed Quail with Collard Greens, Bacon, Hominy, and Black-Eyed Pea Relish

(Serves 4)

For the quail glaze:

1 cup molasses
⅓ cup red wine vinegar
⅓ cup balsamic vinegar
1 cup soy sauce
1 small knob of fresh ginger, peeled and lightly pounded with the back of a chef's knife
3 cloves garlic, crushed
2 shallots, thinly sliced
1 tablespoon red pepper flakes
1 tablespoon whole black peppercorns
1 small bunch of fresh thyme sprigs, tied with kitchen string

For the black-eyed pea relish:

4 tablespoons canned black-eyed peas, drained
2 tablespoons each minced red, green, and yellow bell peppers
2 cloves garlic, minced
4 tablespoons extra-virgin olive oil
2 teaspoons finely chopped fresh chives
Salt and freshly ground black pepper to taste

For the hominy:

1 15.5-ounce can cooked hominy
2 tablespoons cream
Salt and freshly ground black pepper to taste

For the collards:

½ bunch (about 10 leaves) collard greens, rinsed
    and stems removed
4 slices smoked bacon, diced
Salt and freshly ground black pepper

For the quail:

4 quail, ribs and spines removed (or you can serve
    2 birds per person)
Salt and freshly ground black pepper

To prepare the glaze, combine all of the ingredients except the thyme in a medium saucepan and bring to a boil over high heat. Add the thyme, then remove from the heat and allow the mixture to steep until cool. Strain, discard any solids, and set aside. (The glaze can be prepared several days in advance and stored in a covered container in the refrigerator.)

Prepare the black-eyed pea relish by combining all ingredients in a small bowl. Season to taste with salt and pepper. Set aside.

To prepare the hominy, drain off all but 2 tablespoons of the liquid. Puree hominy and reserved liquid in a blender or food processor until smooth. Place in a small saucepan and stir in the cream. Season to taste with salt and freshly ground black pepper. Place the saucepan in a larger pot one-quarter full of gently simmering water (also known as a water bath) to heat through, stirring occasionally. (Don't be afraid to add a little more cream if the hominy seems too thick. If it's at the right consistency, it should "stand up" on a spoon.)

Stack the collard leaves on one another and roll into a cigar-like bundle. Cut down the length of the bundle, snipping ⅛-inch-thick shreds. (This is known as making a chiffonade.) Heat the bacon in a large skillet over medium heat to cook and to render the fat. When crispy, remove and drain the bacon on paper towels, reserving 2 tablespoons of the fat to cook the collards. Add the collards to the hot pan, and sauté over medium heat for just 1 minute, stirring to coat. Season to taste with salt and pepper.

Ask your butcher to remove the quails' spines and rib cages but to keep the leg bones intact. To prepare, heat a gas or charcoal grill to medium heat. Soak the quail in the glaze for 2 minutes, remove, and season lightly all over with salt and pepper. Cook to medium; count on roughly 3 minutes per side, depending on the size of the quail.

To serve, place about ½ cup of the hominy puree in the center of four plates. Top with the warm greens and then the quail. Scoop a few tablespoons of the black-eyed pea relish off to the side. Using a spoon, arrange the relish into a short, fat line for garnish.

Robert's of Charleston

182 East Bay Street, downtown
(843) 577-7565
www.robertsofcharleston.com
Owner: Robert Dickson
Chef de Cuisine: MariElena Raya

Robert Dickson credits Julia Child and Simone Beck for his adeptness in classical French cooking. He befriended Child while he was at cooking school, once visiting her while she hand-corrected the first edition of *Mastering the Art of French Cooking.* A lifelong mentor, Child helped Robert and a chef friend find apprenticeships in kitchens around France. After a series of cooking positions in this country, he opened Robert's of Charleston in 1976, back when Charleston was in a relative culinary infancy.

Despite the city's sharpened competitive edge, Robert's continues to thrive as much for its delicious food (now prepared by Robert's daughter MariElena) as for its delightful music. Robert, a gifted baritone opera singer, struts his stuff around the intimate dining room while singing stirring renditions of Broadway hits like *Oklahoma!, South Pacific,* and *Camelot.* It's more fun than the best-ever party and as romantic as moonlight and roses. Consequently, Robert's is always a big hit for special occasions.

Like her father, MariElena embraces classical technique in the restaurant's five-course prix fixe dinner menu, but she likes to keep it as modern and fresh as possible. Take, for example, the restaurant's popular roasted breast of duckling, which she pairs with an innovative butternut squash sauce.

Pistachio Roasted Duck Breast with Butternut Squash Sauce
(Serves 4)

For the duck breast:

4 Muscovy duck breasts
½ cup white wine
2 teaspoons finely chopped fresh thyme leaves
Salt and freshly ground black pepper to taste
½ cup finely chopped unsalted pistachios

For the sauce:

1 tablespoon butter
1 small butternut squash, peeled, seeded, and cut into ½-inch cubes
1 cup white wine
1 tablespoon chopped shallot
1 tablespoon chopped fresh sage leaves
2 cups heavy cream
Salt and freshly ground black pepper to taste

Preheat the oven to 375°F. Place duck breasts fat side down on a sheet pan, spacing evenly. Pour the wine over the breasts and sprinkle with thyme, salt, and pepper. Press the chopped pistachios into the breasts with your palms; the moisture from the wine helps them stick. Roast the breasts for 15 minutes, or until they have an internal temperature of 150°F (medium rare). Remove from the oven and allow to cool completely. Trim the fat from the breasts with a paring knife. Slice the breasts thinly and at an angle. Press them together and reserve until ready to reheat. Reserve all drippings from the roasting pan for the sauce. Increase the oven temperature to 425°F for reheating the duck after the sauce is complete.

To prepare the sauce, melt the butter over medium heat in a medium saucepan and add the squash, tossing to coat. Cook until tender, 15 to 20 minutes. Add the drippings from the duck roasting pan. Increase the heat to high, add the wine, shallots, and sage, and reduce by half. Puree the mixture in a blender until smooth and, using a fine-mesh strainer, strain into a clean saucepan. Add the cream and bring to a boil over medium-high heat, stirring. Season to taste with salt and pepper.

Return the sliced duck to a sheet pan and reheat in the oven for 5 minutes. Fan several slices of the duck on a plate and dress with the warm sauce. At Robert's, MariElena pairs this with roasted squash risotto and roasted matchstick root vegetables.

Just Desserts

Maybe they're all on a sugar high or have visions of sugarplums dancing in their happy heads, but the chefs featured in this sweet chapter are surely a contented and whimsical lot. Their joy shows up in their smiles and their confections.

At 181 Palmer, admired chef and instructor Scott Stefanelli composes a Reese's-like blend of peanut butter and chocolate mousse served on a chocolate/coconut cookie crisp. See Wee's old-fashioned, homespun appeal delights in a thick coconut cake dressed with a fluffy seven-minute frosting honed to perfection by Amy White. Huck's Lowcountry Table's Kara Hollstein dares to blend caramel popcorn with custard to create her buttery, crunchy Caramel Popcorn, while Matt Lewis and Renato Poliafito's engaging energy electrifies downtown's Baked and powers its heady brownie bombs. No one could resist the playfulness of Cupcake's Kristin Kuhlke's S'mores Cupcake, a nectarous ode to childhood and campfires.

181 Palmer

CULINARY INSTITUTE OF CHARLESTON/TRIDENT TECHNICAL COLLEGE
—PALMER CAMPUS
66 COLUMBUS STREET, DOWNTOWN
FOR RESERVATIONS (REQUIRED): (843) 820-5087, EXT. 2
WWW.CULINARYINSTITUTEOFCHARLESTON.COM
CHEF: SCOTT STEFANELLI AND STUDENTS

If it weren't situated on a campus and if the servers and cooks weren't so young, you'd swear you were at a five-star restaurant. In fact, you are in a live culinary classroom at 181 Palmer, where the advanced-level hospitality and culinary students work the stations of a real restaurant to prepare for real-life work. It sounds serious, but these kids have a ball. The servers, clad in black and with notepads in hand, exude joy and enthusiasm. It comes through in the food, too. Beautifully presented and impeccable, it's proof that this kitchen is 100 percent on.

Veteran chef and long-term instructor Scott Stefanelli is at the center of it all. This living laboratory gives him an opportunity to do what he loves most—teach. "I like being a chef and teaching for the same reason. Both jobs give me a chance to mentor," he says. Scott creates a new menu for each semester—spring, fall, and summer—that revolves around seasonal produce and core techniques he aims to teach. The results are divine—Skillet Oyster Stew, Grilled American Shrimp with Cauliflower Puree, Capers and Currant–Brown Butter Vinaigrette, and on and on—and the public is invited! One of the best deals around, the restaurant offers a three-course lunch for a low cost, sweet tea and white linens included.

Reservations are required, either by phone or online, and 181 Palmer closes for a brief time between semesters. Visit the Web site for schedule and menu updates.

This Reese's-Cup-on-culinary-steroids recipe employs two different mousse-making techniques and features an engaging interplay between cool and crunchy. The bananas are a warm garnish and are prepared just before serving.

PEANUT BUTTER AND MILK CHOCOLATE MOUSSE WITH COCONUT CRUNCH AND CARAMELIZED BANANAS
(Serves 12)

For the coconut crunch:

¾ cup heavy cream
1½ cups finely chopped dark chocolate
1 cup flaked coconut, toasted until lightly brown
½ cup finely chopped hazelnuts, toasted
2 cups crumbled French waffle cookies or
    Piroulines

For the chocolate mousse:

2 cups small pieces milk chocolate
½ stick (4 tablespoons) unsalted butter
3 eggs, separated
1 tablespoon water
¼ cup granulated sugar
1 teaspoon vanilla extract
1½ cups heavy cream

For the peanut butter mousse:

2 cups heavy cream
3 gelatin sheets or 1½ teaspoons
    powdered gelatin
4 eggs
½ cup powdered sugar
1½ cups good-quality peanut butter

For the caramelized bananas:

4 large bananas, peeled and sliced into rounds
Juice of ½ lemon
¼ cup dark rum
½ stick (4 tablespoons) unsalted butter
¼ cup brown sugar

Special equipment: an 11-inch springform pan,
    cooking spray

First, prepare the coconut crunch. Spray the
springform pan lightly with a cooking spray like
Pam. In a medium, heavy-bottomed pan, heat the
cream over high heat until it comes to a boil. Put
the chocolate in a medium bowl and pour the hot
cream over it. Stir until the chocolate has melted
completely. Fold in the remaining ingredients and
mix just until the chocolate has coated everything.
Press the mixture into the bottom of the
springform pan and spread evenly. Refrigerate
until ready to fill with the mousse.

To make the chocolate mousse, put the
chocolate and butter in a large bowl and place
over a gently simmering water bath. Melt gently
and slowly, stirring. Remove from the heat to cool
slightly, but do not allow the ganache to harden.
Meanwhile, combine the egg yolks, water, sugar,
and vanilla in a medium bowl over the same
simmering water bath and whisk vigorously until
thick ribbons form, about 4 minutes. Fold this
mixture into the ganache. In a medium bowl, whip

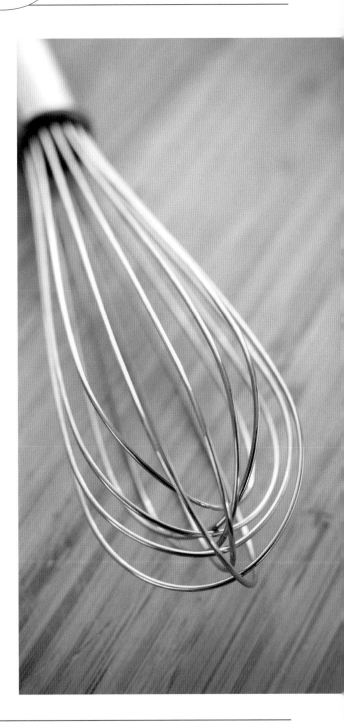

the egg whites with a handheld blender or whisk until soft peaks form. Fold the egg whites into the chocolate mixture. (Scott says, "the mixture may seem grainy at this point, but fear not, it will come together.") In a medium bowl, whip the cream with a handheld blender or whisk until peaks form. Gently fold the whipped cream into the chocolate mixture, then gently transfer the mixture to the prepared springform. Tap the pan lightly on the counter until the mousse is level. Cover with plastic and refrigerate for at least 2 hours before proceeding.

To prepare the peanut butter mousse, heat 1 cup of the cream in a small pot over medium-high heat to bring to a simmer. Remove from the heat and add the gelatin. Whisk gently to dissolve. Set aside, keeping warm enough to prevent the gelatin from setting. In a medium bowl over a simmering water bath, vigorously whisk together the eggs and powdered sugar until thickened. (The mixture should form thick ribbons and have the smooth, liquid pudding weight of a sabayon sauce.) Cool immediately by placing the bowl over a larger bowl filled with ice water. Stir to facilitate the cooling process.

Whip the remaining 1 cup of cream in a medium bowl with a handheld blender or whisk until soft peaks form. Place the peanut butter in the bowl of a mixer fitted with the paddle attachment. Turn the mixer on at low speed and gradually add the cream and gelatin mixture until completely incorporated. Scrape the sides of the bowl with a spatula to make sure the peanut butter is fully incorporated. Remove the paddle, scraping off any excess peanut butter mixture and returning it to the bowl. Fold in the warm egg and sugar mixture by hand. With a spatula, gently stir in one-third of the whipped cream. Fold in the remaining cream, gently, in two parts. The mousse should have a smooth, fluffy consistency. Spoon the peanut butter mousse on top of the chocolate mousse in the springform pan. Spread evenly and tap the pan to level it. Refrigerate, covered with plastic, for at least 4 hours, but preferably overnight. (The mousse can also be frozen in the springform pan for several days and thawed in the refrigerator before serving.)

Just before serving, prepare the bananas. Toss the banana slices with lemon juice and rum in a medium bowl. Set aside. Heat a medium sauté pan over medium heat. Add butter and sugar and cook until the sugar is dissolved and the mixture begins to bubble. Add the bananas and heat through, about 5 minutes.

To serve, gently unmold the mousse and slice into wedges as you might a cheesecake. Serve a wedge on each plate with a few slices of warm bananas and their sauce alongside.

SEE WEE RESTAURANT

4808 HIGHWAY 17 NORTH, AWENDAW
(843) 928-3609
WWW.SEEWEERESTAURANT.COM
OWNER: MARY RANCOURT

Before it became a restaurant, this roadside bungalow was a general store known as See Wee Supply. About thirty miles north of downtown, it's neatly nestled between the sprawl of Mount Pleasant and the fishing village charm of McClellanville, a little farther up the road. It has drawn hungry travelers and lovers of hush puppies, fried seafood, and killer cakes for nearly twenty years, happily with no signs of stopping or slowing down its steady stream of good eats and rural allure.

True to her plan, Rancourt kept all the general store kitsch when she transformed the store into a restaurant and culled a mix of family recipes (what she calls "good home cooking") to create the simple yet satisfying menu. Her sister, Amy White, and sister-in-law help with baking the cakes and pies for which See Wee is known. See Wee's Old-Fashioned Coconut Cake is Amy's baby and, accordingly, she speaks of it with love. "It's something that's evolved through trial and error. I finally got it to just where I wanted it. It's the soft seven-minute frosting that makes it so good," says Amy.

A dandy of a cake, it's not too sweet, it's full of moisture, and it's See Wee's longstanding best-selling dessert.

SEE WEE'S OLD-FASHIONED COCONUT CAKE
(Serves 8)

For the cake:

1 stick (¼ pound) unsalted butter
1½ cups granulated sugar
2 eggs, plus 2 egg yolks (reserve the whites for the frosting)
2 cups self-rising flour (White Lily)
1 cup milk
1 teaspoon vanilla extract

For the frosting:

1½ cups granulated sugar
1 teaspoon cream of tartar
Dash of salt
2 egg whites
⅓ cup water
½ teaspoon coconut extract

For the garnish:

2 cups dried coconut flakes

Special equipment: two 9-inch cake pans

Preheat the oven to 350°F and bring all the cake ingredients to room temperature. Cream together the butter and sugar in a large bowl with a hand mixer at medium speed, until frothy and light. Add the egg yolks and beat for 2 minutes to combine. Add the whole eggs and repeat. Turn the mixer to its slowest speed and slowly add the flour and milk to the batter, alternating ¼-cup quantities of each. Finally, blend in the vanilla.

Grease and flour both cake pans and pour the batter into them, tapping to level the cakes. Bake for 25 minutes or until the cake springs back to the touch. Remove from the oven and cool for a few minutes. Run a flat spatula around the edges of the pans to loosen the cakes. Turn them out onto cooling racks and allow to cool completely before frosting.

To make the seven-minute frosting, prepare a boiling water bath over high heat in a large pot. Combine all ingredients except the coconut extract in a medium heatproof bowl and beat with a hand mixer on high speed over the warm water for exactly 7 minutes—hence the name. Be sure not to let the bowl touch the boiling water; it should sit just above it. Amy says the frosting will be "very fluffy and stand in peaks." Remove frosting from the heat and fold in the coconut extract.

To prepare the coconut for the cake, place it in a food processor fitted with a steel blade and pulse 3 to 5 times. Amy insists this makes the cake easier to slice and serve.

To frost the cake, working on a cake stand, frost the top of the bottom layer of the cake generously and sprinkle generously with the coconut. Top with the second cake layer, frost the top generously, and sprinkle generously with the coconut. Frost the sides of the cake and, cupping the coconut in the palm of your hands, press the coconut into the sides.

From here, slice, serve, and eat!

HUCK'S LOWCOUNTRY TABLE

1130 Ocean Boulevard, 2nd Floor, Isle of Palms
(843) 886-6772
WWW.HUCKSLOWCOUNTRYTABLE.COM
Pastry Chef: Kara Hollstein

When she was a little girl, Kara Hollstein's meal attention wasn't focused on breakfast, lunch, or dinner. "None of these were as important to me as what we got for dessert," says the jovial young pastry chef. "My mom told me I paid good attention to detail. I thought maybe I could become a pastry chef. I went to school and everything seemed to fit," says Kara.

Pastry and Hollstein do fit, indeed. Huck's classic yet whimsical menu of Lowcountry dishes like Cinnamon Rum Brined Bone-In Pork Chop and Oysters Rockefeller Pasta and the beachy backdrop on the Isle of Palms (referred to by locals as "IOP") fits Kara's "simple but classy" style like a glove.

She takes particular pride in her ice creams, all of which she prepares from scratch. Huck's patrons all scream for her original Caramel Popcorn Ice Cream, a creamy, crunchy cool custard with "super buttery" caramel popcorn mixed in and served on top. "When I first came up with the idea, I was worried because I thought that when someone bit into the ice cream it might hurt their teeth. But that doesn't happen because when it's frozen, the caramel softens a little bit because of the moisture," explains Kara.

Have fun with this one. Kara does. She's plated the ice cream in many ways, including in a spun caramel nest and sandwiched between chocolate cookies. At home, a few scoops in a bowl dressed with a caramel popcorn garnish will work just fine.

CARAMEL POPCORN ICE CREAM
(Makes 1 quart)

For the ice cream:

1¼ cups heavy cream, plus more if needed
¾ cup whole milk, plus more if needed
½ cup granulated sugar
1 tablespoon light corn syrup
1 tablespoon vanilla extract
1 bag popped "extra buttery" microwave popcorn
   (Kara suggests Orville Redenbacher's)
8 egg yolks

For the caramel popcorn:

1½ cups granulated sugar
1 bag popped "extra buttery" microwave popcorn
   (Kara suggests Orville Redenbacher's)
Pinch of kosher salt

Special equipment: ice cream maker

To prepare the ice cream, combine the heavy cream, milk, ¼ cup granulated sugar, corn syrup, and vanilla extract in a large sauce pot and bring to a boil over high heat, stirring to combine. The second it comes to a boil, remove it from the heat and stir in the bag of popped popcorn. Set aside and allow the mixture to steep and absorb the popcorn flavor for 20 minutes, stirring occasionally. After it's steeped, strain the mixture through a fine sieve or chinois, discarding the solids. Measure the strained liquid. You're shooting for a total of 2 cups liquid. If what you have is shy of that amount, add equal parts heavy cream and milk to get there. Return the liquid to the sauce pot and bring to a boil over medium-high heat, being careful not to scorch.

Combine the egg yolks and the remaining ¼ cup sugar in a large bowl. Whisk vigorously until the mixture is frothy, light, and lemon yellow in color. As soon as the milk mixture reaches a boil, whisk it, in a slow and steady stream, into the egg and sugar mixture. Whisk until thoroughly incorporated, then return the mixture to the pot. Cook the custard mixture over medium heat, whisking constantly, until it reaches 180°F and coats the back of a spoon. (Be careful here. If the custard gets too hot or if you stop whisking, you could end up with a pot of sweet scrambled eggs.) Remove the custard from the heat, strain through a fine-mesh sieve or chinois, and refrigerate in a covered bowl overnight.

Meanwhile, prepare the caramel popcorn. Prepare an ice bath in advance, combining a large bowl of ice with a bit of water, to stop the caramel from cooking once it's prepared. In a medium sauce pot, heat ¾ cup sugar over medium-high heat. Once it's melted, add the remaining ¾ cup sugar. Stir gently with a flat-edged wooden spoon, being careful not to burn the sugar. The sugar is caramelized when it has turned a dark amber or light to medium brown color. At this point, remove the pot from the heat and immerse it in the water bath for 5 to 10 seconds. Remove from the bath

and stir in the popcorn, gently stirring to fully coat. Pour the popcorn out onto a parchment-lined sheet pan and spread out with a wooden spoon. Sprinkle lightly with kosher salt. When it's moderately cool (but not cold) remove the popcorn from the pan, breaking it into individual kernels and discarding any unpopped corn.

To finish the ice cream, freeze the cooled custard according to your ice cream machine's instructions. After it's done setting up in the machine, stir in the caramel popcorn, reserving 1 cup for garnish. Return the ice cream to the freezer to harden. When it's reached ice cream consistency, serve. Place 2 or 3 scoops in each bowl and drizzle with the reserved caramel popcorn.

BAKED

160 East Bay Street, downtown
(843) 577-2180
WWW.BAKEDCHARLESTON.COM
OWNERS: MATT LEWIS AND RENATO POLIAFITO
PASTRY CHEF: PATRICK PANELLA

A few years ago, when dynamic duo and pastry fanatics Matt Lewis and Renato Poliafito were working together at an ad agency in New York, they forged a dream of opening a pastry shop. But a different kind of pastry shop. Inspired by the likes of French pastry great Pierre Hermé and others, they envisioned a pastry shop with clean, unfettered lines and gorgeous, tasty treats. "There is a horrific sameness to many pastry/coffee shops around this country. All the ones we saw had lace curtains and pie tins. To us, American desserts like brownies and chocolate chip cookies are just as important and wonderful as French and Italian desserts. Too often, here, they get dumbed down," says Matt.

Enter Baked, first in Brooklyn and now in Charleston. The pale orange tiles and white and honey-toned woods speak of a new kind of pastry shop, but the food tells the delicious story. Bundt cake gets a bubbly lift from Coca-Cola, white cake is infused with malt, and chocolate cake is kissed with Oreo crumbles. Voilà, the new American pastry shop! Pastry chef Patrick Panella was imported from the Brooklyn shop to oversee Charleston's Baked kitchen. Though most recipes are created by Matt and Renato, Patrick is putting together a strategy to get more tarts and pastries utilizing fresh, seasonal Southern fruits on Baked's menu.

This brownie is confession-worthy, what with its buttery, chocolate decadence. It's turned a few heads already—including the folks at *O* magazine, who have given it best brownie honors. The main thing is to not overstir the batter. "That's the secret to a good brownie," declares Renato. This recipe was originally published in Matt and Renato's cookbook *Baked: New Frontiers in Baking*.

BAKED BROWNIES

(Makes 24 brownies)

1¼ cups all-purpose flour

1 teaspoon salt

2 tablespoons dark unsweetened cocoa powder

11 ounces good dark chocolate (60–72% cacao), coarsely chopped

2 sticks (½ pound) unsalted butter, cut into 1-inch pieces

1 teaspoon instant espresso powder

1½ cups granulated sugar

½ cup firmly packed light brown sugar

5 large eggs, at room temperature

2 teaspoons vanilla extract

Preheat the oven to 350°F. Butter the sides of a 9 x 13-inch glass or light-colored metal baking pan.

In a medium bowl, whisk the flour, salt, and cocoa powder together. Put the chocolate, butter, and espresso powder in a large bowl and set it over a saucepan of simmering water. Stir occasionally, until the chocolate and butter are completely melted and smooth. Turn off the heat, but leave the bowl over the water. Add the sugars. Whisk until completely combined, then remove the bowl from over the water. The mixture should be at room temperature. Add 3 eggs to the chocolate mixture and whisk until just combined. Add the remaining 2 eggs and whisk until combined. Add the vanilla and stir until combined. Do not over-beat the batter at this stage or your brownies will be cakey.

Sprinkle the flour mixture over the chocolate mixture. Using a spatula (not a whisk), fold the flour mixture into the chocolate until just a bit of the flour mixture is visible.

Pour the batter into the prepared pan and smooth the top. Bake in the center of the oven, rotating the pan halfway through the baking time, for 30 minutes or until a toothpick inserted into the center comes out with a few moist crumbs sticking to it. Let the brownies cool completely, then cut into squares and serve.

Tightly covered with plastic wrap, the brownies keep at room temperature for up to 3 days.

Cupcake

433 King Street, downtown
(843) 853-8181
www.freshcupcakes.com
Owner: Kristin Kuhlke

When Kristin Kuhlke is looking for new flavors for her precocious little cakes, she knows exactly where to go—the grocery store. "I like to walk down the aisle at the grocery store to get cupcake ideas from ice cream flavors. Rocky road, mint chocolate chip, you name it, they work," exclaims the perky entrepreneur.

Though Cupcake puts out diminutive cakes from behind its brown and pink polka dot walls, Kristin's business concept was, in fact, ice-cream driven. The Neapolitan—vanilla, chocolate, strawberry—color scheme and soft serve–like wisps of frosting that top each cake here provide ample proof.

Cupcake serves a total of forty flavors, including chocolate peanut butter, mint chocolate chip, lemon blueberry, and cookies 'n' cream, rotated seasonally. A select nine are served each day of the week. S'mores recalls happy childhood memories of summer campfires. Note that the icing contains a lot of sugar, which helps get the lift and stiffness required for Cupcake's signature swirl, later dipped (like an ice cream cone) in chocolate.

S'mores Cupcakes

(Makes 20–24 cupcakes)

For the cake:

2½ cups cake flour
2½ teaspoons baking powder
1 teaspoon salt
2 sticks (½ pound) butter, at room temperature
1¾ cups granulated sugar
3 eggs
2 teaspoons vanilla extract
1 cup milk
1 cup semisweet chocolate chips

For the icing:

2 sticks (½ pound) butter, at room temperature
1½ teaspoons vanilla extract
½ cup Marshmallow Fluff
9 cups sifted powdered sugar
½ cup milk
⅓ cup graham cracker crumbs

For the chocolate ganache dip:

½ cup half-and-half
2 cups semisweet chocolate chips

For the garnish:

1 cup mini marshmallows
Graham crackers broken into sticks

Preheat the oven to 350°F. To prepare the cake, mix together the flour, baking powder, and salt in a large bowl; set aside. Separately, beat the butter and sugar together in a large bowl until fluffy. Add the eggs, one at a time. Add the vanilla and mix well. Gradually fold in flour mixture with a spatula, adding a little at a time, alternating with the milk. Fold in the chocolate chips. Scoop the batter into two muffin pans lined with cupcake papers using an ice-cream scoop. Bake for 18 to 24 minutes or until a toothpick inserted in the center of a cupcake comes out clean. Remove from the oven and cool cupcakes on a pastry rack.

Meanwhile, prepare the icing. Beat the butter in a large bowl with a handheld mixer until fluffy. Add vanilla and Marshmallow Fluff. Slowly add the sugar and milk, beating at medium speed,

alternating adding small portions of each. Beat in the crumbs at low speed. Using a pastry bag with a rounded tip, ice each cooled cupcake with a generous swirl of icing (approximately 2 tablespoons each). Line the cupcakes up on a baking sheet and refrigerate for 15 to 20 minutes to set the icing.

To prepare the ganache, heat half-and-half in a small saucepan over medium-high heat until it just begins to simmer. Place the chocolate chips in a medium bowl and pour the hot half-and-half over them. Stir with a wooden spoon until the chips are melted and the mixture is smooth and creamy. Let cool for 5 to 10 minutes. Turn each cupcake upside down and dip briefly in the ganache. Top each cupcake with a few mini marshmallows and pierce with a graham cracker stick.

Index

About the Author

Holly Herrick is a former restaurant critic and features writer at Charleston's daily newspaper, *The Post and Courier*. She is a classically trained chef with a Grande Diplome from Le Cordon Bleu Paris and a graduate of Boston College. A first-place nationally awarded food writer by the Association of Food Journalists, she is the author of *Southern Farmers Market Cookbook* and has contributed articles to *Southern Living, Gourmet, Food & Wine, Charleston Style and Design,* and several Southern regional publications. She lives in Charleston with her chocolate cocker spaniel, Tann Mann, and her tortoiseshell cat, Chutney. For more information or to contact Holly, visit www.hollyherrick.com.